Children in the Church?

Betty Pedley and John Muir

National Society/Church House Publishing

National Society/Church House Publishing
Church House
Great Smith Street
London
SW1P 3NZ

ISBN 0 7151 4885 0

First published in 1997 by The National Society/Church House Publishing

© *Betty Pedley and John Muir 1997*

Photocopying

Permission is granted for photocopies to be made by the purchaser for use within their organisation of the specific 'photocopiable pages'. These can be found on the following pages: 20, 24–7, 29–30, 34–5, 40–41, 44, 47, 50, 52, 62–3, 64–5, 66–7, 69–70, 75–6, 80, 83–5, 89–91, 96–7, 101–2, 105–7, 110–11, 115–18, 122–6, 128–32, 146, 149, 153–4, 158, 160, 163, 166, 169, 172, 175.

Cover design by Lee Barnes

Page design and typesetting by Church House Publishing

Printed by The Cromwell Press, Melksham, Wilts.

Contents

Acknowledgements

The authors and publisher gratefully acknowledge permission to reproduce copyright material in this book, as indicated in the list below. Every effort has been made to trace and contact copyright owners. If there are any inadvertent omissions in the acknowledgements we apologise to those concerned.

Numbers refer to page numbers in this book.

The Central Board of Finance of the Church of England.
The Alternative Service Book 1980: 99–100, 104, 133–5 *Patterns for Worship*: 86.

Diocese of Chelmsford Council for Education and Training.
From *Patterns for Worship*. Used by permission: 93.

Jubilate Hymns.
From *Church Family Worship*. Prayers by Michael Perry are in copyright and are used by permission of Jubilate Hymns: 77, 78, 82, 87 (amended), 88, 93, 94 (amended), 99 (amended), 103, 104 (amended), 113, 114, 120-21.

Scripture Union.
From *A Church For All Ages*. Used by permission: 78, 79, 81.

Stainer & Bell Ltd.
Extra verses of 'Think of a world'. Copyright © Doreen Newport. Reproduced by permission: 95.

The Right Reverend Nigel McCulloch, Bishop of Wakefield.
Diocesan Children's Charter: 176. Reproduced by permission.

Thanks are also given to the following for their contribution to this book:

The Wakefield diocesan working party on the behaviour of children in the church, for their help and support.

The congregation of Sowerby Parish for helping to test out many of our ideas.

Michael Perham, author of *Lively Sacrifice* (SPCK, 1992), for his insights into the liturgy.

Preface

My only disappointment with *Children in the Church?* is that it was not available thirty years ago when I was setting out as a parish priest. It is a publication of the highest order, imaginative, well-informed, enabling its readers to grow through interaction with its presentation. Our Lord said that unless you become as a child you cannot enter the kingdom of heaven: this book amply shows us how to treasure the contribution children can bring to the Church's worship and life. I warmly commend it without hesitation in the knowledge that those who read it will find their faith, worship and outlook tremendously enriched.

David Hope, Archbishop of York

Key to resources

OH   Overhead slide for projection during the service

OHP   Overhead projector

A&M   *Hymns Ancient and Modern Revised,* The Canterbury Press, 1981.

ASB   *The Alternative Service Book 1980*

CFAA   Peter Graystone and Eileen Turner, *Church for All Ages,* Scripture Union, 1993.

CFW   Michael Perry (ed.) *Church Family Worship,* Hodder & Stoughton, 1986.

CMP   Peter Horrobin and Greg Leavers (eds), *Combined Mission Praise,* Marshall Pickering, 1990.

JP   *Junior Praise* (songs 1–300 from Book 1; songs 301–503 from Book 2), Marshall Pickering, 1986, 1992.

LP   David Peacock (ed.), *Let's Praise,* Marshall Pickering, 1988.

PFW   *Patterns for Worship,* Church House Publishing, 1995.

Introduction

How can a church make children and their families feel welcome? This is one of the most important questions facing the Church today. It is a question that we have been struggling with in recent years, both in our particular ongoing parish situation, and on a wider level in more than 175 parishes in our particular diocese. This book arose out of our experience of looking for answers to this question. We became aware of how desperate the need is in some situations, and the variety of problems that need to be tackled: poor facilities; lack of understanding of, and sometimes downright hostility towards, the needs of children and young families; lack of leaders, or leaders who feel they are floundering; bewilderment at the changes in the way today's children think and live.

It quickly became clear that with all these different needs, and with the very different situations in different parishes, there was no one 'package' that anyone could produce that would provide the instant solution. What was needed was a tool to help parishes find the answers that would suit them in their own situation. We designed sheets which posed challenging questions. These were used to help people in the parishes to see there was a problem, or what was the *real* nature of that problem. Practical worksheets were produced to help tackle the problems identified. From this collection of leaflets, and the experience gained in sharing them with parishes, this book began to emerge.

A key event in the thinking of the Church of England about this whole question was the publication of the book *Children in the Way* in 1988. This report did much to encourage and develop people's thinking about the rightful place of children in the full life of the Church. The pun in the title (it could either mean are children 'in the way'? – i.e. just a nuisance; or are children 'in the Way'? – i.e. fellow-travellers with adults following Jesus who is the Way) helped people identify the problem facing the Church.

It recognised that in recent years the picture of the Church as a family has been very prominent. The advantage of this is that it recognises our interdependence, that children learn by imitation, that there should be sharing, and that children are recognised as important. But it also has limitations: it can seem exclusive, and appear to leave out single and elderly people.

Instead of the 'family', *Children in the Way* preferred the word 'household', which is rather wider in meaning, and less exclusive than 'family'.

Perhaps more radically, *Children in the Way* also said that we need to think of the Church as people on a journey of faith. It asked us to imagine the Church as a group of people of all ages on a walk. They might walk at different speeds. The children may go at different speeds, following their curiosity. But the group is united in its goal of where the walk is leading to, and the general direction to follow. This picture of the Church is described as the 'pilgrim' model. The implication of this idea is that adults and children are fellow-learners, who have much to learn *from each other*. But it also means that adults are models which children will follow (for better or worse!). *Adults have therefore to provide a leadership worthy of the children.* One person is quoted: 'I don't remember what I was taught. But I do remember some of the people who taught me.'

The 'pilgrim' model of the Church does not mean that we do not need special facilities and special leaders for our children. But the report says that if the Church only sees the work of children's leaders as removing children out of the way of adults, both the children and their leaders (as well as the whole life of the Church) are being devalued. Nor does the 'pilgrim' model diminish the role of parents: in fact it enhances the role of parents as leaders. What becomes clear is that the members of the Church have to *be as Christ* for the children, and this is far more than just telling a few stories to keep them quiet!

This may be all right in theory, but what happens in practice? Clearly, even though many hundreds of hours have been spent on the discussion of child-related issues in recent years, practice is very varied, sometimes good and sometimes bad. From our experience we can list ten bad things and ten good things. We have called them 'Ten for sorrow' and 'Ten for joy'.

'IN THE WAY …'? — TEN FOR SORROW

Examples of *bad* practice that we have discovered or experienced.

1. Noisy and disruptive children present a challenge to the Church, and many churches need help in dealing with this situation positively. But in many churches, parents have been told to 'go home' or leave their children at home.

    Adults and children leave the church.

2. One man phoned us to share the rejection he and his small children had experienced in church – and also to register the prejudice he had experienced from within the church, being a man caring for (his own) small children.

    Adults and children feel they have to change churches, or leave altogether.

3. In one church, feeling against the presence of children was so strong that separate services had to be held – one with children and one without!

    What kind of situation is this for nurturing children and inviting newcomers?

4. In many churches, the attitudes to children's behaviour are so extremely liberal and permissive that it is driving adults away. For instance, in one church we have seen a child being allowed to hurl hassocks from the pulpit at the congregation during the service without being checked.

    Adults leave the church.

5. Often without thought, children are excluded from what is happening:

    - they are not given books or service papers because they might not be able to read;
    - they are not given hand candles for celebrations at Easter or Candlemas;
    - they are made to sit at the back where they cannot be seen (and where they cannot see) so that they are not a distraction.

    Children get fed up with this and leave; parents then stop at home with them; parents frequently put the needs of their children before their own, and if the children don't want to go to church, parents don't go either.

6. Children are put in groups into rooms that are not fit for children to be in. Some are dirty, piled high with flower vases and Oasis, and dusty, out-of-date books. They are dull, often cold and cramped.

    Children will not come and parents should not send them into these situations.

7. Churches are refusing to accept that children have much to give, and will not even allow their pictures to be displayed in the church. Children's work is excluded from the offering of gifts within the service of Holy Communion.

   Children who are not valued and respected for who they are soon drop off – and parents with them.

8. We have been told in a good number of parishes: 'Oh, there is no work for you here. We're not a children's church,' or, 'We're a church that doesn't want anything to change.'

   Children and their parents are not expected to attend.

9. Others say: 'We don't want a crèche because even if the door is closed we might hear a baby crying.'

   Baptism families stop at home until their children are older, or in fact never come back at all.

10. There are many places where regular worshippers stop at home because they do not want to be in church if children are present throughout the service – or if there is to be a baptism.

    The Baptism Service says 'We welcome you' – do we?

'IN THE WAY ...'? TEN FOR JOY

Examples of *good* practice we have discovered or experienced.

1. Churches work with thousands of children during Lent, Holy Week and Easter. In our diocese, we estimate that 40 per cent of those children are not regular members of Junior Church or church congregations.

   Outreach and nurture need to go hand in hand.

2. In those churches, hundreds of adults and older teenagers are involved in running and leading the Holy Week and Easter events.

   All ages are sharing together.

3. We know a church which had only a handful of children two years ago, but now has real problems on a Sunday morning because there are so many children they do not have room for the growing numbers. Our

latest information from this church is that for part of the service they have to use the common room in the nearby almshouses.

Good organisation, preparation and planning, and a commitment to mission are bringing in the people.

4. Holiday clubs continue to be a major focus for many churches, enabling churches in our diocese to work with over 2,000 children during the summer holidays. Each year several churches run a holiday club for the first time.

People are trying different approaches – 'cast your net on the other side of the boat'.

5. Nationally there is much talk of decline, but our experience is that new groups are opening up for under-5s, Sunday morning work, after-school activities and 11–14s work.

Children are responsive when the approach is relevant and lively.

6. Adults are undergoing serious training, including one-year courses, in order to develop their own skills and understanding, but also exploring the role of being advocates for children in their parishes.

Ongoing training is a crucial part of our work.

7. Some parishes have very good practice in their children's work, and are willing to use their experience to help others who are struggling.

People are sharing good practice across the diocese.

8. More ecumenical groups and events are being tried, and some are proving very successful.

The Body of Christ includes all denominations.

9. Parishes are seeking training and advice with regard to all-age worship and all-age learning events. A number are exploring some very imaginative programmes including workshops and worship.

More people are thinking 'all-age'.

10. Parishes are paying more attention to children in worship, and not concentrating all their efforts on parallel activities.

However, good as these things are, there is absolutely no room for complacency while there are so many negative things happening, and examples of children and their families being actively turned away from our churches.

Both before and since the publication of *Children in the Way*, many books have been written about children and the Church. Some are purely theological and philosophical studies which explore the place of children in the Church and in the kingdom of God. Others are very practical books, which deal with age-appropriate uses of the Bible, approaches to prayer with children, and suggestions for interesting and exciting activities and games.

This book is not intended to be another similar book to add to such a collection. It is written for those churches who do want children to be 'in the Way', but who struggle to put this desire into practice. This struggle is causing some to question if their desires and intentions are right after all. In many churches, both children and adults have had bad experiences when they have tried to worship together. The children have disrupted the adults, and the adults have made their disapproval clear to both the children and to their parents. This book is designed to help clergy, PCCs, and Church policy-making groups to work through the practicalities of their sincere desire to welcome and nurture children in the Christian Faith. It is particularly concerned with the place of children in worship. This involves working with parents to establish a co-operative situation. Much of the noise created by children is the result of adults giving them inappropriate toys to play with (bunches of keys), and by children who are bored as a result of being ignored by their accompanying adults. It is also hoped that this book will challenge the thinking of those churches in which children are clearly 'in the way' to help them become fellow-travellers 'in the Way'.

Chapter 1 looks at *how* we can welcome children of different ages into our worship and is divided into four parts, each looking at a different age-group. We recognise that if the welcome is to be real, it has to be expressed in practical terms. The arrangements and facilities required are different according to the needs of different age-groups, and so the four parts of Chapter 1 explore the practicalities of welcome in relation to four age-groups:

1   Under one year (babies)
2   One–three years (tots)
3   Three–six years (nursery/infant)
4   Seven–eleven years (junior)

Chapters 2 and 3 look at the particular opportunities and problems that arise when we want to welcome and include children in worship planned to accommodate all ages. What do you do when it is a non-eucharistic service, or a Eucharist with a less formal Ministry of the Word? This might be the service many churches call a 'Family Service' or 'All-age Service' or 'Worship Together' (e.g. the Service of the Word). In some churches, this will be the Ministry of the Word in a Parish Communion Service.

Chapter 4 looks at the particular opportunities and problems that arise when we want to welcome children to either part of or to the whole service of Holy Communion, and when the service is being celebrated in the usual 'adult' way.

FIRM FOUNDATIONS

The suggestions embedded in these four chapters are rooted in our biblical understanding of the place of children in the kingdom of God. The Bible leaves us in no doubt that both children and adults are important. It is often argued that some parts of the Old Testament seem to teach that children are to be welcomed mainly for what they will become when they are adults. For instance in Genesis 17.19 the promise of the birth of Isaac is sometimes taken to mean that Isaac was only valued for the promise of the covenant God would make with him. The story of Hannah's desire for a child in 1 Samuel 1 could be taken to mean that Hannah only wanted a child because of her sense of disgrace, so that when she gave birth to Samuel she was quite happy to send him away to Eli at Shiloh.

But perhaps more typically there are other references where children are valued for themselves. In the Garden of Eden, Eve rejoiced that she had given birth to a child 'with the help of the Lord' (Genesis 4.1); Isaiah looked forward to the time when a 'little child shall lead them' into God's kingdom *as a child* and not at some later point in life (Isaiah 11.6). Psalm 8.2 says that 'From the lips of children and infants you have ordained praise', and Jesus quotes these words on the first Palm Sunday.

This was not just vague optimism. In the Passover ritual, when the Jews celebrated their deliverance from Egypt, a specific part was given to children: this was to ask the question, 'What does this mean?' (Exodus 13.14). The children's questions are still an important part of the Passover. It is also very true to life: children's questions can really challenge adults! Michelle

7

Guinness, writing from a Jewish background where she says 'there were never any religious occasions in my childhood that were adult only', is always keen to assert this. In *A Little Kosher Seasoning* she writes:

> We tend to see children as those we do something to, not as those who have something to give to us. We fail to respect their integrity and wisdom. One of the saddest aspects of our humanity is that we forget so quickly what it feels like to be a child. You get patted on the head then ignored.
>
> After years of Kiddush in our home on Friday night, our 6-year-old son bitterly resented being unable to take Communion. 'Why can't I have bread and wine?' he asked. 'The official argument is you are not old enough to understand what it means.' 'Are you?' he asked. (p. 277)

Jesus felt at ease in the Jewish tradition of valuing children. He even went further by saying 'Whoever welcomes one of these little children in my name welcomes me' (Mark 9.36). And contrary to his disciples, Jesus welcomed the children (Mark 10.14), and then went on to make their trusting faith a *condition* of our entering God's kingdom! We can imagine that the adults who had brought those children felt they really had entered the kingdom: a little child really had led each one of them. In how many churches would this happen today?

The stories in Mark 9 and 10 about Jesus and the children tell us that:

- We really must welcome children. If we do not, Jesus will not welcome us!

- To welcome children will often be the way of welcoming parents and households.

- *Attitude* is all important. A church can have all the right policies, excellent teaching materials, beautiful premises, but if the people do not welcome the children, everything else will be in vain.

Jesus also has an important lesson about children and worship. In Matthew's account of Palm Sunday, he tells how when the chief priests and the teachers of the Law saw the wonderful things Jesus did, and the children shouting in the temple area 'Hosanna to the Son of David', they were indignant. 'Do you hear what these children are saying?' they asked him. 'Yes,' replied Jesus, 'have you never read [quoting Psalm 82]: "From the lips of children and infants you have ordained praise."?' Why were the religious leaders so indignant? Because the children did not understand what they were singing? They probably did not understand, but that did not prevent Jesus appreciating their praise. Or was it because they were effectively leading the people to recognise Jesus as Lord and Messiah? In that case why should the chief priests and teachers of the Law worry, unless they recognised the potential of children for such leadership?

Whatever the reason for the anger of the religious leaders, Jesus accepted the children's praise, emphasising that praise does not require adult understanding and maturity before it can be acceptable to God. Children and adults can approach God simply and directly. When Jesus told his followers they must become like children, they perhaps already knew that Jesus spoke to God as 'Abba' (meaning 'Dear Father'). St Paul picks up Jesus' call to become like children when he teaches that the Holy Spirit enables *us* to speak to God in the same way, as 'Abba', Dear Father (Romans 8.15; Galatians 4.6). Picking up this point, J. H. Westerhoff III, in his book *Bringing up Children in the Christian Faith* (p. 18), takes it further when he says (from personal observation): 'Children cry "Abba" naturally, adults have to learn.'

The rest of the New Testament does not tell us much about the attitude of the early Church to children. The book of Acts mentions households coming to faith in Christ (Cornelius, Acts 10; the Philippian jailer, Acts 16). But perhaps this is enough to show the importance of welcoming children: for *their* sakes, for *our* sakes, and for the sake of *our outreach into the community.*

THERE BY RIGHT

This book is written in the firm belief that children are in church in their own right, not just because their being there allows the parents to come. This biblical viewpoint is found in the ASB Baptism Service, where the priest says to the newly baptised child(ren):

> God has received you by baptism into his Church.

And the people all respond:

> **We welcome you into the Lord's Family.**
> **We are members together of the body of Christ;**
> **we are children of the same heavenly Father;**
> **we are inheritors together of the kingdom of God.**
> **We welcome you.**

In *The Book of Common Prayer* Baptism Service the same point is made by the priest:

> We receive this Child into the congregation of Christ's flock ...
>
> Seeing now, dearly beloved brethren that *this Child* is regenerate and grafted into the body of Christ's church, let us give thanks unto Almighty God ... and make our prayers unto him that *this Child* may lead the rest of *his* life according to this beginning.

Most recently, the report of the House of Bishops to General Synod (GS 1212, June 1996, p. 4 para. 13) 'rejects the view that the baptism of an infant is efficacious only in some potential sense pending mature personal re-affirmation of faith'. Children, then, are the Church of the present, not only the Church of the future. So there is absolutely no doubt that the authentic Anglican view is that baptised children are in church *by right*, and not by our permission.

However, Jesus was speaking of un-baptised children when he said 'Let the children come to me.' So the same truth applies to children who are sent to church by their parents, or who wander in off the streets because they have nothing better to do. They are all there *by right*.

It is clearly wrong to reject children. But we have written this book because we believe that it is equally wrong to ignore them and let them run riot. To ignore children is not to welcome them. To allow them to run riot is also to deprive them of a real experience of the kingdom of God. The gospel message is that God has set boundaries to our behaviour, and that when we cross these boundaries we need to turn to him and repent, safe in the knowledge that he will welcome, accept and forgive us. A church that sets no boundaries will deprive children of the chance of grasping the essentials of the gospel. A loving, but firm, church fellowship will allow children to *ex-perience* the gospel long before they can *understand* it. So, in this book, we have sought to introduce strategies to help churches to welcome, include and nurture children. We are convinced that this, far from detracting from, actually enhances adult worship and nurture.

NOT ALL AGREE

However, we are well aware that there will be many readers who, while they may agree with us in theory, in practice have bad experiences of children in church. Many others, who may themselves be convinced of what we are saying, still have much work to do to convince other members of their congregations. There are a lot of people in church who do not like the presence of children. This may be for a number of reasons.

1 Noise

Some people cannot cope with the presence of children, and the noise level that children even in a well-controlled situation will create. Many will accept quite happily the small baby who sleeps or sits quietly on a parent's lap during the service, but do not accept that the same baby a few months later is not content to be so docile! There are churches that seem to accept it as quite normal that parents will stop worshipping in church at the time when their babies become active toddlers. Those churches accept it as inevitable that those parents are unlikely to resume the habit of worship in the foreseeable future. In this Decade of Evangelism we are losing hundreds of people in this way.

Sometimes we cannot blame adults for getting annoyed and frustrated when we see what they have to put up with. We have already mentioned the child who was allowed to hurl hassocks at the congregation. We have also seen children allowed to ride tricycles inside the church, behind the congregation, during Communion. We have seen children throwing tantrums, and being allowed to stay in the body of the congregation, kicking and screaming until the tantrums finally subsided. We have seen children being allowed to make loud recurring noises with keys, toys, items of furniture, without anyone attempting to check them.

On the other hand, if the worship and the facilities made available during worship are designed to involve or occupy children as far as possible, then much of the noise will be wiped out. A lot of noise comes from children who are ignored, bored and repressed, and we have tried to deal with this in the remainder of the book.

We believe that churches cannot rely on parents knowing how to direct their children's behaviour in a church setting. Each church needs to set its own boundaries with regard to what is acceptable and what is not. These boundaries can be made known through attractive 'Welcome to our church' leaflets (we have given an example in Chapter 1). But the church also needs to find responsible adults who will befriend and help parents.

A strange twist to this problem is that adults are often unaware of how much noise they themselves make – before the service, during intercessions, and during the administration of Communion. Adults should be encouraged and shown how to provide good role models of behaviour for children. Some adults actually 'wind up' children in church, giving children the impression that it is clever to be disruptive! However, we readily acknowledge that even in a well-controlled situation, the service cannot (and should not) be silent if children are present.

2   Silence, holiness and reverence

So we have to ask how important silence is in public worship. Sometimes people are expecting too much, or even the wrong things from public worship. For instance they may be looking for an experience that really belongs to a guided retreat, or even just to our own private devotions. Silence in our frenetic world is important, and it is right that the Church should try to provide it by retreats, or more regularly by the early Sunday morning Communion Service, or a quiet late Sunday evening or mid-week service. But our main Sunday worship is corporate rather than individual; it is meant to be a foretaste of heaven. The descriptions of heaven in the early chapters of Revelation are so much like descriptions of the Eucharist in the early Church. And, as that book draws to a climax, the atmosphere is of a great crowd and great noise.

There is, of course, the time of 'silence in heaven', and we may be able to achieve times of silence in our all-age worship. Sometimes we will plan for silence, as when we do something which we hope will create 'awe and wonder'. Other times of silence will tend to be 'magic moments' created spontaneously, perhaps by something a child says or does, and filled by the Holy Spirit.

Some adults also feel that some of the non-traditional practices and suggestions in this book are in themselves irreverent. These may be people who accept that children will not be able to sit quietly all the time, but object to worship leaders encouraging children to move about in some of the ways suggested. Often this is due to a misunderstanding as to why the worship leader is leading in a particular way – i.e. not realising that it has a serious purpose within the context of the act of worship.

Sometimes adult attitudes show a misunderstanding about what holiness and reverence mean. They are not necessarily the same as solemnity. For example, 2 Samuel 6.14 describes King David dancing before the Ark – and his wife despised him for it. In the story of Pentecost in Acts 2 some of those present saw the way the disciples were behaving and concluded 'These men are drunk.' Of course, this could go too far, as 1 Corinthians 11–14 indicates. But the problems Paul was addressing were not so much the noise and confusion as the underlying breakdown in fellowship and mutual caring that were the cause of the disturbances. One modern equivalent could be the disturbance of unruly children when they are not being properly cared for and catered for during worship. Another modern equivalent could equally be the disturbance of 'tut-tutting' and 'dirty looks' from adults who have not yet learned to accept children as 'members together of the body of Christ'.

In the New Testament there are very few references to reverence. In the RSV, 1 Peter 3.15 says: 'Reverence Christ as Lord,' though it is more literally 'make holy', so that the NIV translates it as 'set apart'. It is in the context of keeping calm in the face of persecution; i.e. reverence is about obedience to what you believe is the will of Christ rather than an attitude during corporate worship. By that measure, welcoming children in the name of Jesus is in itself a tremendous act of reverence. Hebrews 12.28 tells us to 'be thankful, and so worship God acceptably with reverence and awe, for our "God is a consuming fire"'. The context is again that of standing firm against persecution and hardship, but the reference to worship is in contrast to the Old Testament and its concept of holiness: 'You have not come to a mountain that can be touched . . . The sight was so terrifying that Moses said, "I am trembling with fear." But you have come to Mount Zion, to the heavenly Jerusalem, the city of the living God' (Hebrews 12.18, 21–22).

3   Untidiness

Some other people will object to the kind of approach taken by this book because they think that things like play bags and clipboards make the church untidy, and are somehow 'unholy' objects in a holy place. This objection has similarities to (2), in that it has to do with our concept of 'holiness', and our answer to it is therefore similar. The New Testament definitely downplays the Old Testament stress on holy objects and holy places. The Temple of the Old Testament was such a holy place, and even had a central Holy of Holies into which only the High Priest was allowed, and then only once a year. But the Gospels tell us that as Jesus died the curtain before the Holy of Holies was torn in two, and Hebrews draws the conclusion:

> Therefore, brothers, since we have confidence to enter the Most Holy Place by the blood of Jesus, by a new and living way opened for us through the curtain, that is, his body, and since we have a great priest over the house of God, let us draw near to God with a sincere heart in full assurance of faith .... Let us not give up meeting together, as some are in the habit of doing, but let us encourage one another. (Hebrews 10.19–22, 25)

In 1 Peter we are led to another conclusion, that the church is *people* not buildings: 'you also, like living stones, are being built into a spiritual house to be a holy priesthood, offering spiritual sacrifices acceptable to God through Jesus Christ' (1 Peter 2.5).

The one time in the New Testament when the disciples tried to create a holy place, on the mountain of the Transfiguration, Jesus firmly stopped them.

So we can conclude that if a church building is in any sense 'holy' it is because of the 'holy people' who worship there – and that includes the children. We should therefore no more object to children's objects being in church than we do to hymn books and hassocks. A child playing at the parents' feet can be holy, but not tidy! However, we are not commending untidiness: the child's toys should be cleared away afterwards, just as the hymn books and hassocks should. Churchwardens and sidespeople have an important role, to be sensitive to the needs of children and to the needs of older members of the congregation, and to try to achieve an acceptable balance.

4   *Vulnerability/anxiety*

Another problem some people experience with all-age worship is that they feel insecure with non-traditional practices. They fear the unpredictable element introduced by the presence of children. They wonder whether the priest will cope and whether the adults in the congregation will cope. If they have had bad experiences in the past, their anxieties will be intolerable. They will resist this feeling of vulnerability.

Again 1 Corinthians can help us. Chapter 14, verses 26 to the end are headed in the NIV translation 'Orderly Worship'. The expectation of this section is that people will be contributing to the worship in a spontaneous fashion, but Paul then goes on to lay down rules to control and channel the spontaneity: 'The spirits of the prophets are subject to the prophets' (v. 32). Inspiration is no excuse for chaos! 'For God is not a God of disorder but of peace' (v. 33). God, whose very nature is to be creative, uses that creativity to produce order and beauty.

Those responsible for planning and leading all-age worship should ensure that everyone concerned understands that there is a clear framework, and that there are well-understood guidelines for what happens, and that it is definitely *not* a case of 'anything goes'.

5   *Planning for spontaneity!*

The assumption behind this book is that there will be very careful thought and preparation, of the actual worship itself and of the provision of facilities to enable the worship to take place. This careful preparation and provision functions like the markings on a games field, defining the limits of what can happen, but at the same time allowing and encouraging spontaneity within those limits. When such preparation and provision is seen to have been done, people will be helped to feel secure in, and therefore not threatened by, all-age worship.

6   *Childish?*

If some people are anxious about the effect of all-age worship on adults, others feel that the whole concept is just pandering to children. It is making things too easy for them, and the modification involved in all-age worship is childish and wrong. This is an important point that must be taken very seriously. However, it is not the whole story.

We must not confuse being *simple* (i.e. uncomplicated) with being *simplistic* (i.e. oversimplified, ignoring the real issues). The parables of Jesus are simple in the sense that they are direct and vivid, but they are not simplistic: they are also extremely profound, and can be understood at a number of levels. Nor are the parables of Jesus easy: they contain truths which challenge us to the limits of our faith. The Good Samaritan is an example. It is at the same time a *simple* story about the importance of helping people, a *profound* analysis of human religiosity and prejudice, and a deeply *challenging* call to sacrificial living.

Ideally, all-age worship, like the parables, should be simple, profound and challenging at the same time. The methods used are very simple: all-age worship at its best is visual, dramatic, symbolic. And when all is said and done, as Michelle Guinness points out, 'Nothing is as potentially liberating as the example of children at home in their church, enjoying worship' (*A Little Kosher Seasoning*, p. 279).

7   *Embarrassment*

Having said that, some elements in all-age worship (for instance, children's action songs) may be embarrassing for some adults. Of course many adults may enjoy the action songs, and it is the experience of many churches that all-age worship has given adults the opportunity to become more relaxed in their own worship. But clearly no adults should ever be *made* to do what they feel is childish. Hopefully, though, they can be encouraged (as fellow-members of the Body) to feel pleasure in the enjoyment of the children, and appreciation of the meaning being conveyed by the song. Jesus' command that we should become like children does not mean that we have got to join in the action songs, but it does mean that we can and must learn from the children as they take part. Probably many adults will tend to feel happier with actions which express feelings rather than narrative. Actions that express feelings will be understood as part of the experience of worship.

8   Non-traditional

Related to the fear of all-age worship being simplistic is the fear that it also means we are losing the beauty and treasure of traditional language. Many people assert that beautiful, traditional language touches deep wellsprings in our being, and that modern, simple, functional liturgical language does not do this. Others think that point of view is unrealistic, and that traditional language simply goes over the heads of many people in the congregation. We tend towards the latter view. Certainly we tend to forget that modern liturgies came into being because of dissatisfaction with the traditional services. This is a complex matter, and there is a real need for serious study of this subject.

Obviously what is envisaged in this book is very different from a 'traditional' Anglican service in which everything seems to be pre-set and totally predictable. However, it is also our belief in writing this book that a more open style of worship, far from being a bad experience, is actually pointing the way to worship in the next century (the hope expressed by the new *Patterns for Worship*).

However, it really does not have to be an 'either–or'. The orders of service in this book have places for more traditional prayers, and can be seen as 'planned bridges' into the more formal liturgy of the Church. Some parishes may want to include more of this kind of material. Many churches have more than one service every Sunday, and so it has to be recognised that this may mean more than one congregation, each with a fairly distinct entity, meeting in the same building at different times.

9   Worship for all

Hopefully children can enable adults to respond in a way they would not have done if children had not been there, and that creates an atmosphere of worship for children in a way that would not be possible if adults were not there, so that there is positive interaction. Small children like to move about and create something which becomes part of the worship (the 'Ooh-aah' factor can be positive in this respect!). The skill of the worship leader is to take hold of what the children have done, and draw on the symbolism to evoke an atmosphere of worship, which in turn will give the children an experience they could not otherwise have had. For example, one church had a Candlemas procession, with an adult carrying a 'baby' escorted by Cubs carrying candles. A very long-standing member of the congregation said afterwards that it was the first time he had *really* understood the Nunc Dimittis (and he must have sung it at Evensong hundreds of times).

While there is obviously a great responsibility laid on the shoulders of the worship leader 'up front', it should not all be left to that one person. We need to help parents, and adults who find themselves near children, to be worship leaders for the children. Clergy are taught that the very act of presenting an act of worship, in a way that draws in the people, is itself worship. That applies to the parents and neighbouring adults of children in church.

So what? So what is *your* church like? Not, it is hoped, like the description by Ishmael (in *Angels with Dirty Faces*) of the imaginary church visited by the imaginary family the Crumbles:

> The doormen remind the children that they are about to enter the house of God, so they must be opposite to everything that God has made them to be: that is, they must keep silent, sit still, and show no external signs of happiness or else they will be dumped back in the Sunday School cells where the children really belong. (p. 139)

We hope this book will help clergy, PCCs and everyone involved in policy-making in the churches:

● to develop a sincere desire to welcome and nurture children;

● to understand *why* this is so theologically right;

● to work through the practical implications of this desire.

The book can be used for individual study or group discussion situations. Particular sections can be used for training. Some pages are especially suitable for this purpose, and can be photocopied or reproduced on OHP slides. A list of these pages can be found at the front of the book.

LET THE CHILDREN COME

Welcoming children and their parents

When thinking about any of the four age-groups in the context of any act of worship, a distinction must be made between

OCCUPATION

and

PARTICIPATION

The balance between these two will change as the child matures. This chapter is divided into the four age-groups.

Under one year (babies)

One–three years (tots)

Three–six years (nursery/infant)

Seven–eleven years (junior)

Each part will consider:

● age-appropriate creative and stimulating *occupation*;

● age-appropriate meaningful *participation in a non-eucharistic service*;

● age-appropriate meaningful *participation in a eucharistic service*.

It is not realistic to expect to engage the attention of a child under 11 years for the length of a service, especially when it lasts for more than an hour. So there will be times when a child is being *occupied*, and times when the child is actively *participating* in the service. The balance between occupation and participation will vary from one service to another, and from one child to another. Some churches operate a policy of withdrawal for part of the service. This will be discussed in the context of each age-group and each type of service.

Whenever we speak of adult leaders for groups of children, we assume they have been properly appointed according to the Code of Practice of the diocese to which the parish belongs.

Babies

(Under 1 year)

If babies are brought into the worship in our churches, what might we expect?

- prams and buggies in the aisle

- babies sleeping

- babies gurgling and chuckling

- babies crying

- babies being fed

- parents walking about at the back of the church

Welcoming babies

How can we help to make these babies and their parents feel welcome and relaxed?

OCCUPATION

1 Crèche

Some churches provide a crèche facility in a separate room ('withdrawal model'), where babies and young children are cared for by properly appointed, responsible members of the church (and/or parents) on a rota basis. Parishes operate different policies with regard to this type of facility. Some present the use of the crèche as very desirable and to be encouraged; whereas other parishes encourage parents to keep a child in the service for as long as possible, and only take him/her to the crèche when the need arises.

If a crèche situation exists:

- the service can be relayed into the crèche through speakers so that leaders are still part of the service and the children absorb something of the atmosphere of the service;

- leaders should be responsible, loving *adults*. Teenage helpers have an important role to play, but should never be left unsupervised or have the full responsibility for the young children;

- there should be a good selection of clean, well-maintained, safe, appropriate toys;

- the room in which the crèche meets should be clean and warm, and free of any potentially dangerous furniture and fittings;

- children are never too young for simple finger rhymes and songs. The choice of books, use of mobiles etc. can be part of a church's nurturing policy for the under-fives, and this can include items suitable for babies of this age.

- If it is not possible or desirable to have a separate creche, facilities within the church should be provided. Some churches choose to have these facilities in addition to the crèche so that there is full parental choice.

2   A carpeted area

This is an area where an older baby can be put down to move about safely and quietly.

The baby needs to have a selection of specially chosen, quiet toys and books.

The baby should always be under the supervision of an adult who can control the noise, but who is able to encourage older babies to be involved in some parts of the service through appropriate play activities.

3   Play bags

To help under-ones feel happy, content and at home in church, it is a good idea to have play bags available. These are bags containing toys, activities and books suitable for the age-group. To make the bags, a pillowcase or two tea towels sewn together can be used with a drawstring added, or a bag can be sewn from any brightly coloured material.

For play bags to be used successfully, they can be given out by the sidespeople to young families *as they arrive*. This says to the family:

Welcome!

We are ready and waiting for you and your child(ren).

We want your child to feel he/she belongs here.

We want this service to be a good experience for you all. (Parents are happy if their children are happy and contented.)

It can be a very negative experience if a bag is only produced once a child is struggling and fretful. This can be an intimidating experience for the parents.

Suggested contents for the babies' play bags

A selection of soft toys (a range of different fabrics in each bag adds interest and variety: fur fabric, velvet, felt, knitted wool, etc.). Often in a congregation there are people who will knit and sew toys for the bags if asked.

●   Plastic baby toys (be sure they do not squeak or make a noise!).

- Board books (very thick cardboard pages) and bath-type books with plastic 'chewable' pages. There are many beautiful books of this nature with biblical themes. Don't use books with ordinary pages as these can get torn and spoiled and this is stressful to parents and other members of the congregation who are nearby.

You can use anything that is appropriate to this age-group that is:

- colourful and attractive;
- ready to be used and played with and not just good to look at;
- most of all, quiet!

Warning

Play bags need checking and replenishing. Toys should be washed regularly. There is nothing more disappointing than a bag full of broken toys and torn books. This is a job for someone in the church to take on. It cannot be left to chance. This person might also be given suitable items for the bags.

4 Nappy-changing facilities

These could be located in the toilets.

5 An attractive leaflet

This can explain to new families the facilities for babies and small children. This should clearly state that it is OK to get up and walk about at the back of the church with a baby who will not settle. Or it may indicate where in the building a parent can go to take the child until he or she is settled. This area needs to be warm and have a comfortable chair. Trying to settle a baby in a cold, dark porch does not help anybody. Do not recommend that a parent takes the baby to join the children's group. If the baby is disrupting the worship, he or she will disrupt the children's group too. An example of such a leaflet is given on the following pages.

CHILDREN IN THE CHURCH

Welcome!

to you and your child

Your child in our church

When children are baptised, we say: *'We welcome you into the Lord's family'*.

Children are never too young to come to church. At church we belong to one big family. We want you and your children to know that you are all **very welcome**.

We do realise that bringing children, especially babies and toddlers, to church can be very hard work . . . i.e., if a baby cries, yours is always the loudest (or so it seems at the time!).

If toddlers get restless and want to walk about or do something different, the minute you try to stop them, the more determined they become and start trying to get away.

We do want coming to church to be a joyful experience for you and your child. Inside this leaflet you will find some information which we hope will make your being in church easier and more enjoyable.

You and your baby

If your baby is settled, please feel free to remain seated, even if others are standing.

If your baby cries loudly he/she needs:

- feeding

- changing

- a lot of comfort (often assisted by being carried around, talked to, sung to etc.).

Don't be embarrassed if your baby cries. We all understand that babies have special (and urgent!) needs. A baby who is crying needs help. If you just try to stop him/her crying it usually gets worse, you become stressed and embarrassed, others can't hear, and it is hard work for the person leading the service.

These facilities are provided for you and your baby's convenience and to help your coming to church to be a happy, relaxed experience for you and your baby:

- a comfortable chair to sit in while feeding your baby can be found at the back of the church by the coffee area;

- changing facilities are available in the toilet area.

If you need to walk around to settle your child, please feel free to do so at the back of the church.

How to help your baby enjoy being in church

Feel free to bring quiet toys for your baby to hold.

Some babies may be attracted by the colours of stained-glass windows, or the flicker of candles. If they are near, point them out to your baby.

Babies may well find pleasure in being held close as a parent sings, and in hearing the music of the services.

Older babies may watch active, dramatic parts of the service. Tell them when something different is happening.

If it is a service of Holy Communion take your baby with you to receive God's blessing at the time of Communion.

Already your baby is absorbing the atmosphere of worship, and so starting on the journey of faith.

You and your toddler

A service can feel like a long time for a pre-school child.

- He/she can have some quiet toys or books in the pew. These are to be found in the carpeted crèche area by the font. The pews by this area are also carpeted.

- If he/she needs more space, go with your child to this carpeted area.

- **In the interests of safety as well as quietness, children should always be accompanied by an adult.**

We all understand that young children cannot be still for very long, but they can move around on the carpet and play with quiet toys without making much noise at all.

Children are likely to be noisy, or to want to run around. Please discourage this where possible, and distract them with the toys and books available.

The facilities we've provided are to help coming to the church to be a happy, relaxed experience for you and your toddler.

How to help your toddler enjoy being in church

Children learn by imitation. Encourage your toddler to imitate what the adults are doing: holding a book and standing on the seat beside you 'singing', kneeling down, or sitting at prayer times.

Encourage your toddler to respond to the music by moving or clapping when there is a strong rhythm.

If it is a service of Holy Communion take your toddler to receive God's blessing at the time of Communion.

Remember

Children who are allowed (or even encouraged) to run around during the service are not so much being included as ignored! They are present in worship as part of their own faith journey. Even when they are just amusing themselves they are absorbing the atmosphere of worship, but we should also be seeking ways of involving them and drawing their attention to what is going on in the worship, even if it is only for a few minutes: 'Watch!' 'Listen!' etc.

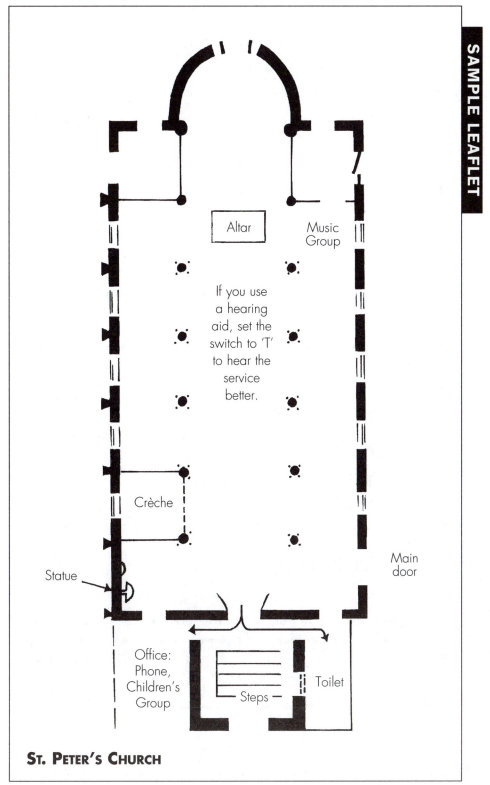

Altar

Music Group

If you use a hearing aid, set the switch to 'T' to hear the service better.

Crèche

Statue

Main door

Office: Phone, Children's Group

Steps

Toilet

St. Peter's Church

PARTICIPATION IN A NON-EUCHARISTIC SERVICE

- Babies may well find pleasure in being held close as a parent sings.
- Some babies may be attracted by the colours of stained-glass windows, or the flicker of candles.
- Older babies may watch active, dramatic parts of the service.
- Babies will respond to welcoming smiles from members of the congregation.

(For more details see Chapter 2.)

PARTICIPATION IN A EUCHARISTIC SERVICE

- Babies may well find pleasure in being held close as a parent sings, and in hearing the music of the services.
- Some babies may be attracted by the colours of stained-glass windows, or the flicker of candles.
- Babies will be taken by their parents to receive God's blessing at the time of Communion.
- Older babies may watch active, dramatic parts of the service, especially if they have a colourful impact.
- Babies will respond to welcoming smiles from members of the congregation.

(For more details see Chapter 4.)

The person leading the worship cannot realistically engage the attention of babies in the service. But adults accompanying children can do a lot to help their children join in the worship. They become the worship leaders for the children, and their own worship is enhanced by doing this.

Challenge

If a parent has a crying, fretful baby in your church, what do they have to do?

- Sit it out, much to the frustration and annoyance of many in the congregation.

- Go and stand in a cold, dark porch.

- Walk about outside, often in the pouring rain.

- Go home early.

- Sit on a comfortable chair in a warm vestry, crèche, or parish room.

What happens in *your* church? Write in your answers and discuss with other people concerned.

Tots

(1–3 years)

This is by far the most difficult age to integrate a child into the worshipping life of the church. With children of this age, what might we expect?

They will have:

- a very short attention span;

- an inability to be still for more than a few seconds;

- a developing use of language;

- a love of running about;

- an ability to make a lot of noise;

- a very strong will.

And they will:

- learn through their senses;

- imitate others;

- have no sense of time;

- believe what they are told.

Welcoming tots

How can we help to make these tots and their parents feel welcome and relaxed?

OCCUPATION

1 Crèche

See the section on babies (under 1 year). However, there will be opportunity for further development of structured, nurture-type activities.

2 A carpeted area

This is an essential for children of this age. They must have space and opportunity to move about safely and quietly. Without this facility, children can be noisy, disruptive, bored and waiting to get out and go home. But note:

● A good, appropriate selection of toys puts the church in a strong position for encouraging/insisting that children play with the church's toys, if the ones they have brought from home are noisy and unsuitable.

● Children should *never* be allowed to go to this area alone. To allow this is not only likely to lead to noise, but to the child falling and being hurt. Although parents should be encouraged to accompany their children to this area, there should still be a properly appointed adult supervisor.

Many parents allow the children to bring very inappropriate toys to church. Quiet toys are not easy to find, because toys for children of this age are made to stimulate their senses. It is a very specific job for someone in the church to collect and maintain suitable toys for use in church.

3 More carpet

If the church has wooden or stone floors, it is a good idea to put some carpet runners on the floor in the pews where young children and their families are encouraged to sit. If the children run about, the carpet helps to deaden the sound of their footsteps. This is further helped by encouraging parents to remove children's outdoor shoes and replace them with slippers. If carpet runners are placed along the pews also, this cuts down the noise of toys and books on the woodwork.

4 Play bags

These can have more different toys than the bags that are intended purely for the young babies. Bags are probably most useful with children of this age. Parents should be encouraged to produce one thing at a time from the bag. This ensures that the interest is maintained. If all the contents of the bag are tipped out in the first few minutes of the service, interest in the toys will be exhausted before it has been really useful.

5 An attractive leaflet

This can explain the facilities for small children to new families. (See previous example on pages 24–7.)

6 A potty in the toilets

PARTICIPATION IN A NON-EUCHARISTIC SERVICE

Children of this age have a very limited attention span, but they can be drawn into the service in different ways for a few minutes, then allowing their attention to stray to the contents of the play bags, before drawing it back again to the flow of the service.

● Have some music which has a rhythm to which young children can clap or shake simple home-made percussion instruments.

● Have some flags with the words 'Thank you' written on. Invite children to wave their 'Thank you' flag at the end of a thank you prayer, or during an appropriate song or chorus.

● As part of the sermon slot have items hidden or placed around the church. Invite parents and young children to go and collect them. This gives a creative and meaningful opportunity for moving about.

● Have as many visual things as possible. Children need to be able to see, to hear, and to be able to respond in a participatory way.

- Encourage children to imitate the worshipping adults and older children.

- Children respond to being known by name and to people talking to them.

(For more details see Chapter 2.)

PARTICIPATION IN A EUCHARISTIC SERVICE

At this age children learn by imitation. Encourage them to imitate what the adults are doing: holding a book and standing on the seat beside the adult 'singing', kneeling down, etc.

- At prayer times, give children a prayer book of their own to hold and look at, e.g. *Sorry* – a 'Talking with God' board book. This can be used at the prayer of Confession. There are also *Thank You* and *Please* books in this series. And there are several books written for this age about the Lord's Prayer. (See Appendix B for details of these books.)

- Children of this age will respond to music of all kinds, but especially to music with a pronounced rhythm.

- Tots will be taken by their parents to receive God's blessing at the time of Communion.

- Tots will respond to people knowing them by name and talking with them.

Remember

Children who are allowed (or even encouraged) to run around during the service are not so much being welcomed as ignored. They are present in worship as part of their own faith journey. In between their periods of playful occupation, we should be seeking ways of involving them and drawing their attention to what is going on in the worship: 'Watch!' 'Listen!' etc.

(For more details see Chapter 4.)

Challenge

If a child aged 1 to 3 years in your church is really noisy, what happens?

- Parents get embarrassed and upset, and vow not to bring their children again until they are older.

- Parents ignore the noise and seem to think it is acceptable.

- Parents take the child home.

- Parents are scowled at and talked about by members of the congregation ('our children *had* to sit still' etc.).

- Parents are encouraged to use the facilities provided.

- Parents are offered help if appropriate.

- Parents are helped to know what is an acceptable level of noise and what is not.

What happens in *your* church? Write in your answers and discuss with other people concerned.

Nursery and Infants

(3–6 years)

If children between the ages of 3 and 6 come into the worship in our churches, we might expect that:

- they are physically small and will not be able to see what is happening;

- their movements are often unco-ordinated;

- fantasy and fact are equally real – their imaginations are developing rapidly;

- their life is centred around home and family, nursery/playgroup, and hopefully church;

- they have limited (but growing) vocabulary and understanding;

- they take everything literally;

- they want to please;

- they imitate others;

- they believe what they are told;

- they love stories.

Children's spirituality

Spiritually growing children aged 3 to 6 may have these characteristics.

1   They experience a growing sense of awe and wonder as they become aware of One beyond themselves.

2   They think of God in terms of their own experience. He is associated with their parents/carers. They think of God as human, with physical characteristics.

3   They begin to love and trust God, and know that he will hear them when they talk to him. They can pray to God at any time, and in any place, and they will pray simple prayers of petition and thanksgiving.

4   They will grow in their desire to please God.

5   They can praise God by giving thanks.

6   They begin to know that Jesus loves children, and they want to love him.

7   They know that the Bible is a very special book which contains wonderful stories of Jesus.

8   They can understand and enjoy selected Bible stories. They will often recall and request favourites.

9   They are beginning to have a concern for others.

10   They are beginning to share, be thoughtful and helpful, and can sometimes relate their actions to a story they have heard.

You may not recognise many of these qualities in children you know, but this list gives some indication of the spiritual potential of children in this age-group.

Welcoming young children and their parents

How can we help to make these children and their parents feel welcome and relaxed?

OCCUPATION AND LEARNING

1 Structured group activities

Just as the under-3s go into a crèche, so many churches have groups for children in the 3–6 age-group, where for part of the service they have the Ministry of the Word delivered in an age-appropriate way.

The kind of material that can be used for this sort of group is listed in the book list in Appendix E on page 183. There is a lot of other material available for the longer sessions of the Junior Church or Sunday school nursery classes, but that is not the subject of this book. The material quoted above is suitable for those children who are withdrawn from a relatively short part of the service (half an hour or less). There are only a few commercially produced resources which link activities for this age-group to the ASB lectionary.

However, some churches are not able, or do not wish to withdraw children into a structured activity group.

2 Pew packs

If children are to remain in the service for the whole of the time, then pew packs can be provided. (Details of how to plan and prepare pew packs are found in Appendix C on page 179.)

Children in this age-group still benefit from:

- a carpeted area to which they can go for five to ten minutes during the service. But it should *not* be in the same area as that used by the babies;

- easy access to toilet facilities;

- being served juice when the adults have coffee;
- being known by name and talked to.

PARTICIPATION IN A NON-EUCHARISTIC SERVICE

- Children of this age will respond to music. They will clap and play simple home-made percussion instruments. This is the beginning of their understanding of an expression of praise.
- Children will join in simple action songs. They will do the actions if they cannot learn the words.
- Children can join in prayers that have a simple response which they can be encouraged to share: e.g. 'Lord Jesus, I am sorry,' or 'Help us to love you.'
- Children will respond to anything visual.
- Children need to be able to move about. They can be involved in coming out to the front, going round the church looking for things etc. as part of the sermon slot.
- Activities can include badges to wear, flags to wave, boxes to open, and models to take home.
- Children can join in with the 'Amen'.
- Children respond to being known by name and to being talked to.

(For more details see Chapter 2.)

PARTICIPATION IN A EUCHARISTIC SERVICE

- Children of this age will respond to music, especially if it has a pronounced rhythm.
- Children will watch processions and activity/drama of any kind if they can see well enough.
- Children can be encouraged to join in the 'Amen', and some may know part of the Lord's Prayer.

- Children can be encouraged to imitate adults when singing and praying.

- Children can have their own picture prayer books to use at prayer times. (See suggestions in Appendix B, p. 178.)

- Children can exchange the Peace.

- Children can receive God's blessing at the time of Communion.

- Children will absorb much of the atmosphere of worship while they are occupied with the activities in their pew packs.

(For more details see Chapter 4.)

Challenge

If a young child in your church is disruptive, what happens?

- Somebody asks the parents to take the child out of the service.

- Somebody asks the parents to keep the child still and quiet.

- One or more people scowl at the child and the child's parents in order to communicate displeasure?

- The parents are offered pew activities and/or other facilities (toys, books, use of carpeted area etc.) for the child.

- The child is invited to use the occupational facilities (carpeted area, play bags, toys etc.) under the supervision of a member of the congregation.

- Nothing happens – the situation is allowed to continue, and to get worse.

What happens in *your* church? Write in your answers and discuss with other people concerned.

Juniors
(7–11 years)

If there are children aged 7–11 in our churches, we might expect:

- children hungry for knowledge and information;

- children who constantly ask 'Is it real?;

- children who find identity in groups. They enjoy clubs, and have a strong sense of belonging;

- children whose ability to read and write is developing rapidly, but who will not cope with many of the reading demands of the service books and hymn sheets;

- children who may come 'programmed' to believe that the service is not for them – that it is boring and for adults only;

- children who may be disruptive (especially by giggling) if they are embarrassed by the demands of the worship made upon them (especially the silence).

Children's spirituality

What spiritually growing juniors aged 7–11 may be like.

1   They enjoy stories. They will begin to read them for themselves, and to relate some Bible truth to themselves. They want very definite information about God.

2   They feel a natural love for Jesus, and have a growing sense of a personal relationship with Jesus and with God.

3   They recognise that they have hard times and need to pray about them. They have rapidly developing consciences and are growing in their understanding of sin and forgiveness.

4   They make distinctions between what they are told and what they experience.

5   They have some reasoning power which can be used in learning and adopting spiritual truth.

6   They have ideas about acceptable behaviour, but are not always consistent.

7   Their thinking is still largely concrete and fact orientated, and so they prefer 'yes' or 'no' answers to moral issues.

8   They can be challenged to co-operate and be objective about themselves and their behaviour.

9   Prayer can become very meaningful and a real source of strength and blessing.

10   They need help from Christian adults when dealing with their emotional reactions to situations, behaviour and the way they have been treated by others.

You may not recognise many of these qualities in children you know, but this list gives some indication of the spiritual potential of children in this age-group.

OCCUPATION AND LEARNING

1 Withdrawal groups

As children get older, they are going to be able to participate in more and more of the worship of the Church. However, many churches choose to withdraw children for at least part of each service. Children are withdrawn into groups or classes.

If this is the model being used, it is important that what is prepared for the children is part of a thought-through nurture strategy, and not just a means of occupation which is not linked to the worshipping body of adults.

2 Clipboards

In many churches, children stay in church through an essentially adult service. Within such services there are periods of time when children in this age-group need occupational/learning material of their own, because a particular part of the service is inappropriate to their level of thinking and participation.

Clipboards can be prepared – usually giving material relating to the theme of the day. These can be collected by the children during the hymn before the Gospel, and used during the sermon and administration of Communion. It is important that they are not used by children at times in the service when they are able to participate fully. It needs a lot of co-operation from the adults to encourage the children to use their clipboards when it is appropriate to do so and to refrain from using them when they can join the adults in worship.

Clipboards can be made from hardboard or rigid cardboard (suggested size 30x25 cm/14x12 ins) and strong bulldog clips. Pens, pencils, felt pens can be kept in plastic (clip-top) freezer bags or pencil cases.

The Gospel of the day (whole story or text) can be explored using pictures to colour. Imaginative material can also include puzzles, mazes, word-searches, simple jigsaws, simple action models, games to make and play at home, stickers, badges, bookmarks and prayers. Parts of the Holy Communion Service can also be the subject of these activities.

Questions to ask when considering the use of clipboards

1 Why are we thinking of introducing clipboards? What are our aims for this development?

2 How do we choose the themes for our material? Will it be the theme of the service, or relate to the liturgy itself?

3 Where can we obtain suitable material?

4 How are we going to organise the production and collation of the material?

5 How is this development going to be introduced to (a) the children? (b) the congregation? How do we encourage participation and interest of the congregation in the children's activities?

6 How can we display good things produced by the children?

7 What age range are we to supply material for? Age/ability can vary a lot. How well do we know the children – their reading levels, motor skills, etc.?

8 In which parts of the service are clipboards to be used? For what part of the service are we supplying materials?

9 Will Bibles be available for children aged 7–11 years for use in conjunction with their activities?

10 Will the clipboard activities lead to follow-up material at home (which could be brought back the following week), occasional competitions, displays in church?

PARTICIPATION IN A NON-EUCHARISTIC SERVICE

To encourage as much participation as possible we should seek to make the service:

● SIMPLE (*not* simplistic or childish)

● USE SENSES (watch/listen/touch/taste/smell etc.)

● INTERACTIVE.

We must remember that even in this age-group:

● children have a relatively short attention span

● many of them are not fluent readers

● they need permission to move about. This can be a creative part of the service.

We are seeking to deepen and enrich their experience and understanding of the different elements of worship:

● praise and thanksgiving

● confession and absolution

● hearing and receiving God's Word

● intercession

● offering ourselves to God's service

● seeking God's grace.

For more details see Chapter 2. Many of the ideas can be adapted for use in eucharistic and non-eucharistic settings.

PARTICIPATION IN A EUCHARISTIC SERVICE

Because of their developing attention span and reading ability, children will be able to participate in the worship in an ever-increasing and hopefully deepening way.

- Some children will be able to follow some, if not all, of the service in its printed form. They will need help with finding the place in the text, especially when paragraphs and pages are missed out. Small print and big numbers ('page 867' or 'hymn 592') are difficult for the younger children in this age-group. For children to cope with a service book, they will need a lot of adult support.

- The sermon can include visual aids of different kinds.

- The words of the liturgy can be enhanced by adding visual impact. This intensifies their meaning for children (and adults).

- The special children's service books are strongly recommended. They can, however, be a complication if a particular church takes the service in a different order to that given in the book. (This particularly applies to the prayer of confession.) This can be overcome by attaching a coloured flag to the page of sections which come in a different place. The President can then say 'Turn to the page with the orange flag', etc. The appropriate and stimulating use of these books also requires adult support.

See Book List in Appendix B, p. 178, and for more details see Chapter 4.

Challenge

If there are children aged 7–11 in your church:

- Are there special arrangements/provisions made for them?

- Are they expected to behave and react like adults?

- Are they encouraged to be part of duty rotas etc. alongside adults?

- Are they fidgety and disruptive?

- Are they bored and disinterested?

- Are they quiet?

- Are they rebellious?

How is your church thinking through issues relating to the welcome and creative integration of juniors into the congregation? Write in your answers and discuss with other people concerned.

ALL-AGE WORSHIP

Introduction

WHAT IS 'ALL-AGE WORSHIP'?

This might be the service many churches call a 'Family Service' or 'All-age Service' or 'Worship Together'(e.g. the Service of the Word). In some churches, this will be the Ministry of the Word in a Parish Communion Service.

When we talk about all-age worship, we are *not* talking about children's worship at which adults are present either as participants or as tolerant spectators.

Children's Service with adults present	✗

When we talk about all-age worship, we are *not* talking about the usual adult worship, but with children present throughout.

Adult Service with children present	✗

We *are* talking about a very special quality of worship which can only happen because all ages are present. Some parts of the service can be tackled differently because children are present to enable it to happen. The response of the adults in worship creates an environment for the children's worship which could not have happened if the adults had not been there. The age-groups interact creatively and worshipfully.

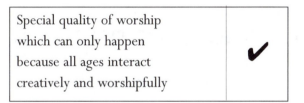

Special quality of worship which can only happen because all ages interact creatively and worshipfully	✔

CAN WE DO IT?

In 1994, the General Synod of the Church of England approved 'A Service of the Word', which gives us an authorised structure for an All-age Service in a non-eucharistic setting. This can be used as an alternative to Morning and Evening Prayer on a Sunday (e.g. a Family Service), or it can be combined with the Ministry of the Sacrament in the ASB service of Holy Communion, in effect replacing the first part of the Holy Communion Service, the Ministry of the Word. The Service of the Word is incorporated into the recently published *Patterns for Worship*.

This authorised service may at first sight appear rigid, but it actually encourages considerable flexibility. This can include readings being dramatised, sung or read responsively, the sermon may include less formal exposition, the use of drama, interviews, discussion and audio-visuals, and hymns or other sections of the service being inserted between parts of the sermon. Details of what is allowed can be found on pages 13–17 of *Patterns for Worship*.

Chapter 3 consists of services which have all been used in parishes in the Diocese of Wakefield, and are built on this structure. The structure is overleaf.

THE SERVICE OF THE WORD

THE PREPARATION

1   The minister welcomes the people with a liturgical greeting.

2   Authorised Prayers of Penitence are used here or in The Prayers.

3   Venite, Kyries, Gloria, a hymn, song or a set of responses may be used.

4   The Collect is said either here or at section 9.

THE MINISTRY OF THE WORD

This includes:

5   Readings (or a reading) from holy Scripture.

6   A psalm or, if occasion demands, a scriptural song.

7   A sermon.

8   An authorised creed or, if occasion demands, an authorised Affirmation of Faith.

THE PRAYERS

These include:

9   Intercessions and thanksgivings.

10   The Lord's Prayer.

THE CONCLUSION

11   The service concludes with a liturgical ending.

This chapter explains how we have developed a strategy for planning all-age services which uses the structure of the Service of the Word. In the following chapter eleven more sample orders of service are then given to show how this has worked in practice.

Planning orders of service for all-age worship

The planning of all-age worship can be a very creative and exciting process. It is best tackled by a group of people who share their gifts, skills and insights. However, we are aware that many people spend long hours labouring over their planning, and yet feel they are going round and round in circles, uncertain of what they are trying to achieve. We have tried to develop a nine-step strategy for planning all-age worship which we believe can enrich the planning experience and help to release people's creative thinking.

Step 1

Think of the planning process as the weaving together of several different threads in a unique and interesting way. There are four main threads to the pattern:

Thread One	Elements of worship
Thread Two	Structure of the Service of the Word
Thread Three	Qualities of the presentation of all-age worship
Thread Four	Special considerations for all-age worship when we want to include young children.

Thread One	*Thread Two*	*Thread Three*	*Thread Four*
Elements of worship	*Structure of the Service of the Word*	*Qualities of presentation of all-age worship*	*Special considerations for all-age worship when we want to include young children*
Praise and thanks	Preparation	Simple (but not simplistic)	Short attention-span
Confession, absolution	Word	Engaging the senses	Reading ability
Hearing and receiving the Word	Prayers	Participation	Inability to sit still
Affirmation of Faith	Conclusion	Use of symbols	
Intercessions			
Offering of ourselves			
Receiving God's grace			

Step 2

Start with the *theme* of the worship, and what is to be your main thrust in the presentation of that theme. Write this at the top of the All-Age Worship Planning Sheet 1 which you will find on page 62.

How do we decide on the theme? Many denominations leave this entirely to the discretion of the local church leaders, though they may have suggested schemes, or recommend a lectionary. The Church of England has lectionaries, which are intended to ensure that all parishes have a balanced pattern of Christian teaching. The ASB lectionary gives a theme for each Sunday, as well as for special occasions like saints' days and harvest festival. The proposed three-year lectionary is not thematically based, so worship leaders will need to identify themes from the readings.

The Service of the Word (in *Patterns for Worship*) allows non-eucharistic services to be more flexible. Except for two periods (from the 3rd Sunday in Advent to the 1st Sunday after Epiphany, and from Palm Sunday to Trinity Sunday) the local church leadership is authorised to devise lectionaries to suit local needs.

Step 3

In the planning group, look at the theme and at the Bible readings given, and brainstorm the ideas that arise and sources of material which could be used in relation to this theme. Again using the All-Age Worship Planning Sheet, jot down the ideas in the 'thematic' boxes under the appropriate headings for the Elements of Worship (Thread One). Be sure you include the sometimes neglected last two elements of Thread One – i.e. the opportunity to make a response to the message, and to receive God's grace, strength, help and guidance to carry out that response. Omitting these elements is one reason why people sometimes criticise all-age worship as bland or childish.

Always relate as many things thematically as possible. For instance try to choose hymns and songs that suit the theme rather than simply because they have been requested, or have not been sung for a long time. Look at books like *Patterns for Worship*, *Church Family Worship*, *Prayers for the People* or *Church for All Ages* for thematic prayers.

Step 4

If there are real gaps which cannot be filled naturally and appropriately with thematic material, then look for some general resources for that purpose and jot down your ideas in the 'general' boxes under each heading.

There is no 'general' box in the planning chart for the Word section, as we assume this section will always be thematic. But in the Prayer section, for example, if no special prayer of confession seems particularly appropriate, then you may put the ASB General Confession in the box.

Step 5

When all the ideas are in place, use Planning Sheet 2 on page 63 to transfer them one by one to their place on the Service of the Word structure, bearing in mind how flexible this structure can be (see *Patterns for Worship*, p. 17). Because of this flexibility we have put the two separate sections 'Word' and 'Prayer' into one section entitled 'Word and Prayers'. Using this chart will enable you to check that your material is adequate and balanced, and can be given an approved structure and development. The structure should not be seen as a burden but rather as a helpful means of achieving a real service of worship, and not just a collection of unrelated items.

Step 6

Now we suggest that you adopt our logos (or your own equivalent ones) and use them in the *left*-hand margin of the Service of the Word sheet (p. 63), to check that your planning is using appropriate methods of presentation for a service of all-age worship. Check your planning for these qualities:

SIMPLICITY	(use the logo 🕭)
VISUAL	(use the logo 👓)
TACTILE	(use the logo ✋)
OTHER SENSES	(use the logo ◉)
PARTICIPATION	(use the logo ☺)
SYMBOLS BEING USED	(use the logo ✠)

As you go through your order of service, look for the following criteria:

♠ = SIMPLICITY

All-age worship should not be simplistic and childish, but it should be simple – unsophisticated and uncomplicated. In its directness and simplicity it can be very profound.

As you look at your order of service, ask:

● *Is this item in the service simply presented? Can it be simplified without changing its meaning or effectiveness?*

If you are happy that it is as simple as it can be, use the logo in the margin.

✌ ✋ ✦ = VISUAL, TACTILE, OTHER SENSES (TASTE AND SMELL)

We are a very visual people, but frequently when we cross the threshold of our churches we are bombarded with words, words, words!

In all-age worship, besides the use of very well-chosen words, we aim to use the visual – colour and movement, as well as tactile and other sensory experiences.

> I hear – I forget
> I see – I remember
> I do – I understand. (Chinese Proverb)

Visual

> pictures, friezes, posters, banners
>
> pictures and objects used in 'the talk'
>
> artefacts
>
> stained-glass windows (use of building)
>
> colour (frontals, vestments etc.)

Tactile

> waving palm branches
>
> carrying candles
>
> unrolling scrolls (as in synagogue)
>
> counting Zacchaeus' money
>
> carrying the lost sheep
>
> children in the offertory procession
>
> children laying table at the Eucharist

Other sensory experiences

> tasting bitter herbs at a Passover celebration
>
> smelling the perfume of the woman who anointed Jesus
>
> smelling incense brought by one of the Wise Men
>
> smelling candles and oranges at a Christingle Service.

As you look at your order of service, ask:

● *How many of the senses are being used during this part of the service?*

Use the relevant logos to mark the engaging of the senses.

☺ = PARTICIPATION

Participation is very important in any act of worship, but especially so when we are looking for ways of engaging young children in worship.

As you look at your order of service, ask:

● *In what ways, at this point in the service, are the people actively involved? Can this be increased?*

Use this logo to mark active participation.

✠ = SYMBOLS BEING USED

Symbols enable people of all levels of maturity in the faith to key into the message at their own level.

For example:

'I am the vine, you are the branches, and my Father is the gardener.'

A vine is built at the front of the church with children collecting cardboard leaves and fruit from around the church (i.e. a creative movement which is an integral part of the service). Once the vine is ready, the leader begins to prune the branches and throw them away. This powerful symbolism (very simply presented) may mean to a 4-year-old: 'I helped make a vine in church this morning.' But, the vine the 4-year-old helped to make, the act of pruning and the subsequent silence that ensued can lead a mature Christian into very real penitence.

As you look at your order of service, ask:

● *How are we using symbols to reach people's different levels of experience and maturity?*

Use this logo to show that this kind of presentation is being proposed.

Step 7

Check your planning for these special considerations:

SHORT SECTIONS	(use the logo ⧗)
READING NOT NECESSARY	(use the logo ⊠)
OPPORTUNITY TO MOVE ABOUT	(use the logo ✈)

⧗ = SHORT SECTIONS

Children (and many adults) have short attention spans. They soon get lost in long prayers and sermons. Within all-age worship, the aim is to keep each part of the service to four minutes or less. A change of voice, style, activity will refocus the straying mind. This means that the usual ten- to twelve-minute sermon could be presented in three parts with a related song or an activity coming between the sections. The service should move smoothly from one section to another, like a 'seamless robe', without any unnecessary delays or hesitations.

As you look at your order of service, ask:

● *What is the approximate length of each short section of this service? Are two or more quiet, still sections placed next to each other? If so, can something be interspersed without spoiling the flow?*

⊠ = READING NOT NECESSARY

Much of what we say and sing in church is written down for us to read for ourselves. This is one of the most basic reasons why children are excluded from a lot of worship – because they cannot read the words! Some children are reading well at school, but the satisfactory reading level of a 7- or 8-year-old is light years removed from the reading skill required by much material used in church (small print, thick books, big numbers, long words, spoken quickly, with the print in unpredictable positions on the page, very few pictures, etc.).

In all-age worship, we should endeavour to present substantial parts of the service in ways that are accessible to those who cannot read, or who do not read well.

● Have children learn frequently used prayers such as the Lord's Prayer, or the Collect for Purity (ASB p. 119, para. 3).

● Choose some hymns or songs with refrains, choruses, key words, which can be taught at the time and memorised quickly and easily. The way in which hymns and songs are announced can draw children's attention to the parts where they can join in. Hymns of this sort are marked ⊠ in the orders of service. There is a list in Appendix D.

● Use prayers with responses which can be learned at the time quickly and easily. The response should always be the same within the same prayer. Changes in the wording of responses require reading abilities. Good examples of responsive prayers can be found in the orders of service in Chapter 3.

● Have a cardboard/hardboard symbol raised prominently at the appropriate time as a cue to children that it is now time for them to sing their refrain or line etc. Sometimes the symbols can be appropriate to the season of the Church's year and the theme of the hymn. Sometimes general symbols can be used.

Such symbols should be at least two or three feet high, depending on the size of your church and congregation. For example:

Advent	candle
Christmas	angel, star
Epiphany	crown, gift
. Lent, Passiontide	cross
Easter	flowers
Ascension	cloud
Pentecost	flame/dove
Discipleship	fish
General	fish, cross, dove, happy face

As you look at your order of service, ask:

● *Could I take part in this part of the service if I could not read very well, or not at all?*

● *Are there hymns or songs, with repetition which can be announced, so that children have a bit to sing and an activity can be made out of waiting to join in again?*

● *Do some of the prayers have the same response throughout, so that it can be repeated by those who do not follow the printed word?*

✈ = OPPORTUNITY TO MOVE ABOUT

Small children are not able to sit still for long periods of time, and if we do not provide creative opportunities for moving about as an integral part of the service, we will inevitably have a lot of children moving about in a way that disconnects them from the service, and that can cause a lot of distraction and anguish to others. We can incorporate this need into the planning and structure of the service by asking children to find things placed around the church which are part of the unfolding theme (e.g. collect leaves and bunches of grapes to make a vine).

As you look at your order of service, ask:

 How can we invite children to move around as a creative part of this service?

 Have we included action songs and/or prayers?

Step 8

Then ask, is it really *all-age* worship? Remember how we defined all-age worship at the beginning of the chapter.

● When we talk about all-age worship, we are *not* talking about children's worship at which adults are present either as participants or as tolerant spectators.

● When we talk about all-age worship, we are *not* talking about the usual adult worship, but with children present throughout.

● We *are* talking about a very special quality of worship which can only happen because all ages are present. Some parts of the service can be tackled differently because children are present to enable it to happen. The response of the adults in worship creates an environment for the children's worship which could not have happened if the adults had not been there. The age-groups interact creatively and worshipfully.

This 'special quality' cannot really be put down on paper, but we can at least check that there is 'something for everybody'. This means that as much of the service as possible should be relevant to all ages, and that there should not be too many sections that are mainly helpful only to certain age-groups.

To check this, use the right-hand margin of Planning Sheet 2 on p. 63, and by each item in the service enter the numbers for the age-groups that might be able to relate to that particular item.

The numbers we suggest are:

1 Under 7 years

2 7–11 years

3 12–16 years

4 Adult

This will help you to see clearly if adjustments need to be made to the flow of your service.

Step 9

Finally, once you are happy with the content, flow, presentation and balance of your service, write it out in enough detail to meet the needs of those leading the service, and to enable service sheets or overhead transparencies to be produced if necessary.

At this stage you will also need to produce a list of jobs to be done, things to be made and people to be contacted, before the service can actually be presented.

The following pages give an example of how the ideas from a brainstorming session can become an order of service, which is then checked in the ways suggested above. After we had filled in Planning Sheet 3 (see pp. 64–5) we found we had more than enough material, and as we transferred items to Planning Sheet 4 (see pp. 66–7), we ticked the items we were using.

In this particular brainstorming session we had available: *Patterns for Worship, Church Family Worship, Church for All Ages,* and *Junior Praise.* The abbreviations used on the Planning Sheets and in the sample services which follow in Chapter 3 are listed on p. viii.

ALL–AGE WORSHIP PLANNING SHEET 1

Theme: _____

Main aim: _____

Elements of worship Thread 1	Thematic material	General material
Greeting		
Praise and thanksgiving		
Confession and absolution		
Hearing and receiving the Word		
Affirmation of faith		
Intercessions (including Collect)		
Offering of ourselves		
Receiving God's grace		

ALL-AGE WORSHIP PLANNING SHEET 2

The Service of the Word

Thread 3	Thread 4	THE PREPARATION Thread 2	Age-groups
👆 ᨆ ✋ ☀ ☺ ✠	⌛ ✉ ✈		
👆 ᨆ ✋ ☀ ☺ ✠	⌛ ✉ ✈		
👆 ᨆ ✋ ☀ ☺ ✠	⌛ ✉ ✈		
👆 ᨆ ✋ ☀ ☺ ✠	⌛ ✉ ✈		
👆 ᨆ ✋ ☀ ☺ ✠	⌛ ✉ ✈		
		THE MINISTRY OF THE WORD AND PRAYERS	
👆 ᨆ ✋ ☀ ☺ ✠	⌛ ✉ ✈		
👆 ᨆ ✋ ☀ ☺ ✠	⌛ ✉ ✈		
👆 ᨆ ✋ ☀ ☺ ✠	⌛ ✉ ✈		
👆 ᨆ ✋ ☀ ☺ ✠	⌛ ✉ ✈		
👆 ᨆ ✋ ☀ ☺ ✠	⌛ ✉ ✈		
👆 ᨆ ✋ ☀ ☺ ✠	⌛ ✉ ✈		
👆 ᨆ ✋ ☀ ☺ ✠	⌛ ✉ ✈		
👆 ᨆ ✋ ☀ ☺ ✠	⌛ ✉ ✈		
👆 ᨆ ✋ ☀ ☺ ✠	⌛ ✉ ✈		
		THE CONCLUSION	
👆 ᨆ ✋ ☀ ☺ ✠	⌛ ✉ ✈		
👆 ᨆ ✋ ☀ ☺ ✠	⌛ ✉ ✈		
👆 ᨆ ✋ ☀ ☺ ✠	⌛ ✉ ✈		
👆 ᨆ ✋ ☀ ☺ ✠	⌛ ✉ ✈		
👆 ᨆ ✋ ☀ ☺ ✠	⌛ ✉ ✈		

ALL-AGE WORSHIP PLANNING SHEET 3

Last Sunday after Pentecost

Theme: Being ready

Main aim: *Jesus is constantly coming to meet us in new opportunities and challenges. We must be ready and equipped to meet him.*

	Thematic material	General material
Greeting	Sentence ✔	Greeting: The Lord be with you etc. ✔
Praise and thanksgiving		(CFAA p. 170) God has called us …✔ (JP 180) Oh! oh! oh! how good … ✔ Praise and thank God for his gift of today Praise and thank God for the Church
Confession and absolution	Wasted opportunities (PFW p. 43, 13C7) ✔ (CFW 557)	
Hearing and receiving the Word	Matthew 25.1–13 ✔ Pictures of the 10 bridesmaids. Practical examples of getting ready: holiday – baby – royal visit. Waiting outside overnight for something important to happen. ✔ Oil-lamp shapes – both sides with message on. ✔ Symbolism of oil . ✔ Introductory activities, counting 2 groups of 5.	

Affirmation of faith	(PFW p. 62 0F9) ✔	Baptismal (PFW p. 58, 0F2)
	Thematic material	**General material**
Intercessions (including Collect)	For opportunities to serve ✔ For those who have lost hope ✔ Collect for Last Sunday after Pentecost (ASB p. 745) ✔	
Offering of ourselves	(JP 50) Give me oil in my lamp ✔ (JP 147) Keep me shining Lord ✔ Funeral Collect (ASB p. 308 no. 3) ✔ (CFW 387) Love divine 4	
Receiving God's grace	Use cut-out lamps for personal prayers ✔	

Now transfer the results of the brainstorming to Planning Sheet 4 on p. 66, ticking each item on Sheet 3 as it is transferred.

ALL-AGE WORSHIP PLANNING SHEET 4

THE SERVICE OF THE WORD

Last Sunday after Pentecost

Thread 3	Thread 4	THE PREPARATION Thread 2	Age-group
🖐 icons	⌛ ✉ ✈	OPENING SENTENCE Matthew 25. 13 GREETING	3,4
icons	⌛ ✉ ✈	SONG (CFW 555) Come let us join our cheerful song	3,4
icons	⌛ ✉ ✈	PRAYER Preparing to praise (CFAA 170)	2,3,4
icons	⌛ ✉ ✈	ACTION SONG (JP 180) Oh! oh! oh! how good is the Lord	1,2,3,4
		THE MINISTRY OF THE WORD AND PRAYERS	
icons	⌛ ✉ ✈	MIME Being ready – for what? Mime the following actions; congregation has to guess what actors are getting ready for: (1) Going on holiday; (2) Going on a picnic; (3) Planning to receive a royal visit.	(1),2,3,4
icons	⌛ ✉ ✈	Hide ten cardboard lamps around the church and ask children to find them.	1,2,3,4
icons	⌛ ✉ ✈	KEY WORDS for Gospel	(2),3,4
icons	⌛ ✉ ✈	GOSPEL READING Matthew 25.1–13	(2),3,4
icons	⌛ ✉ ✈	Link Gospel to 5+5 lamps	(2),3,4
icons	⌛ ✉ ✈	SONG (JP 147) Keep me shining, Lord	(2),3,4

SKETCH Waiting outside the hotel	1,2,3,4
CONCLUSION Being ready; not missing opportunities.	(2),3,4
CONFESSION Missed opportunities (PFW p. 43, 13C7)	(2),3,4
ABSOLUTION	1,2,3,4
SYMBOLISM OF OIL Not our effort or resources but God's grace.	(2),3,4
Give out lamps (with response written on).	1,2,3,4
SONG (JP 50) Give me oil in my lamp	(1),2,3,4
AFFIRMATION OF FAITH (PFW p. 62, 0F9)	(2),3,4
OFFERTORY SONG (CFW 556) Children of the heavenly King	2,3,4
INTERCESSIONS Use lamps and caption response.	3,4
QUIET TIME Link with lamps. PRAYER (ASB p. 308 para. 3)	(1),2,3,4
THE CONCLUSION	
SONG (CFW 387) Love divine	3,4
COLLECT for Last Sunday after Pentecost (ASB p. 745)	3,4
BLESSING	1,2,3,4

ANALYSIS

We can now look at the service as a whole, noting the logos we have circled in the two left-hand columns, and come to the following conclusions.

The service has:

- simplicity of presentation, on and off, throughout the service
- visual and tactile experiences
- no opportunity for engaging smell and taste
- lots of opportunity for interaction
- use of symbolism in a couple of places
- short sections throughout
- a lot of opportunity for the involvement of non-readers
- three opportunities for children to move about.

If we feel that is satisfactory, we need to produce a check-list of tasks to be done before the service can be presented, and this outline planning has to be set out as a detailed order of service, still using the framework of the Service of the Word.

SERVICE PREPARATION CHECK-LIST

Before the service:

- Arrange for people to act in the mime and sketch.
- Prepare ten big cardboard lamps, five obviously full of oil and five obviously empty, and stick them in various places round the church for children to find (see templates on p. 69).
- Prepare enough lamps for each person in the congregation to have one (see templates on p. 70).

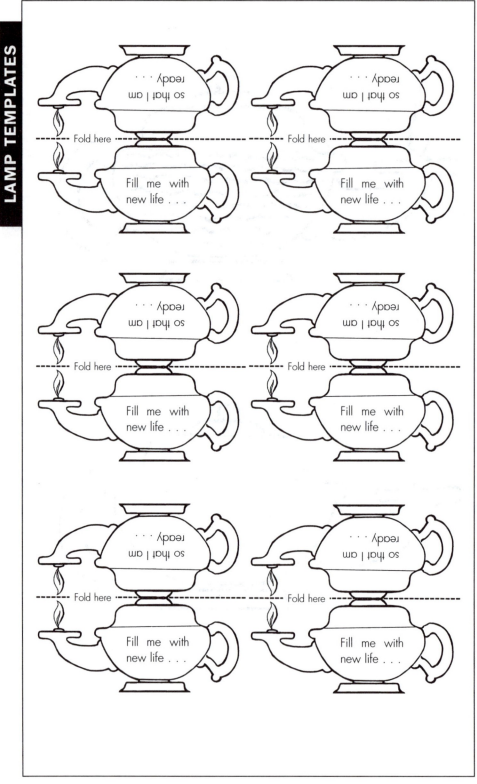

so that I am
ready . . .

Fill me with
new life . . .

Fold here

70

Detailed order of service based on the planning process

THE PREPARATION

Opening sentence   'Keep awake then, for you never know the day or the hour.' (Matthew 25.13)

Greeting   The Lord be with you
and also with you.

Song   (CFW 555) Come let us join our cheerful songs

Prayer   (CFAA 170) Preparing to praise

Action song   (JP 180) Oh! oh! oh! how good is the Lord

Suggest asking people to punch the air, getting higher each time on 'Oh oh oh' and clapping on 'how good is the Lord ... I never will forget what he has' and stamp on 'done for me'. Remember that it is often easier for adults to join in or tolerate actions which relate to feelings rather than those which relate to narrative.

MINISTRY OF THE WORD AND PRAYERS

Mime

Being ready – for what? Two or three people have prepared simple mimes (no words necessary) with props. These should be done with very bold actions and from a place in church where everyone can see. The congregation is asked to guess the situations for which the 'actors' are trying to get ready (packing for holiday etc.).

Key words for Gospel

Explain to the children that we want to be ready to hear the Gospel reading this morning. To be ready we need to find some things to help us. Send them round the church to find the ten cardboard lamps and bring them to the front. Gather the children holding the lamps round the one who is to read the Gospel. Alert the children to the lamps, and ask them to listen to the story.

Gospel reading   Matthew 25.1–13

Link Gospel to 5+5 lamps

Talk about what has been heard. Count the ten lamps and say that some were ready for use and some not. Draw the distinction between the five and the five, and then send children back to places for the song.

Song   (JP 147) Keep me shining, Lord

Sketch

Devise a sketch of a contemporary situation of people waiting outside a hotel all night for the arrival of a special person (pop star/royal visitor/sports personality etc.). Some have come prepared with sandwiches and flasks etc., others have nothing. When those with nothing go to get refreshments from the kiosk, the special person arrives. He is so impressed with those who are waiting that he invites them inside the hotel to have a meal with him. The others return to find they have missed everything. (This idea comes from Sharon Swain, *The Sermon Slot, Year 2*.)

Conclusion

Talk about being ready for all that God wants us to do. Use the sketch and the following talk about not missing opportunities to lead into the confession, giving people time to think about missed opportunities.

Confession and absolution (PFW p. 43, 13C7)

Symbolism of oil

Remind people we cannot be ready for all that God wants us to do by our own efforts. Talk about oil in the Bible as being symbolic of God's love and also his commissioning people to do special tasks. We do not rely on our own efforts but on God's grace.

Invite children to give out to everyone in the congregation small cardboard lamps during the singing of the next song. On one side of each lamp are the words 'Fill me with new life', and on the other 'so that I am ready'. Ask people to hold the 'lamps' with the 'Fill me with new life' facing them.

Song   (JP 50) Give me oil in my lamp

We don't know what God has in store for us, but we step out in faith saying together the Affirmation of faith.

Affirmation of faith (PFW p. 62, OF9)

When the song is over, ask people to hold the 'lamps' with the 'so that I am ready' facing them, and to think about what God gives to us and what we give back to him as a gesture of gratitude.

As a symbol of our confidence in God, we offer him our gifts. This helps to equip our Church to be ready to serve God.

Offertory song (CFW 556) Children of the heavenly King

The collection is taken during this hymn.

Intercessions

Invite people to turn their lamps back to 'Fill me with new life'.

We pray this prayer for ourselves and also for other people.

Have brief intercessions for the Church, the world, those in need. Suggest people say the response as 'Fill *them* with new life'.

Prayer (ASB p. 308 para. 3)

CONCLUSION

Song (CFW 387) Love divine

Collect Last Sunday after Pentecost (ASB p. 745)

Blessing

In the next chapter we give eleven more orders of service, similarly analysed, which have been used in actual parish situations, and which you can use throughout the year. You are free to use or adapt these services – provided you test your alterations in the same way to see if they are appropriate to meet the worshipping needs of your church family. A key to the abbreviations used can be found at the front of the book. We also use the same logos as those given on pages 54 and 57.

SAMPLE ORDERS OF SERVICE THROUGH THE YEAR

KEY TO LOGOS

We use the same logos in these orders of service as in Chapter 2 to help you check that each service is appropriate for all-age worship.

&#128293;	SIMPLICITY
&#12316;	VISUAL
&#9995;	TACTILE
&#9728;	OTHER SENSES
&#9786;	PARTICIPATION
&#10013;	SYMBOLS BEING USED
&#8986;	SHORT SECTIONS
&#9993;	READING NOT NECESSARY
&#9992;	OPPORTUNITY TO MOVE ABOUT

All-age service for Bible Sunday

Thread 3	Thread 4	**THE PREPARATION** Thread 2	Age-group
		GREETING/SENTENCE 2 Timothy 3.16	3,4
✍		PROCESSION with music or hymn	(2),3,4
✍ ✋	⧗ ✉ ✈	*Congregation bring Bibles to front where they are placed on an attractive display. The leader looks at some of the 'special' Bibles.*	1,2,3,4
		Collect for Advent 2 (ASB p. 426)	3,4
✍ ☺ ✠	⧗ ✉ ✈	PRAYER OF THANKSGIVING (CFW 618) *The four words 'Thanks be to God' should each be written on one of four large Bible-shaped cards on sticks and held up by children each time the response is to be said.*	2,3,4
		THE MINISTRY OF THE WORD AND PRAYERS	
		SONG (CFW 609) Spirit of God	3,4
		READING 1) Psalm 119.129–144 2) The power of God's Word: Hebrews 4.12–13	3,4
		SONG (CMP 545) Open our eyes Lord, we want to see Jesus	3,4
✍ ✋ ☺	⧗ ✉ ✈	SERMON *Children unwrap a parcel. It contains (a bottle of) milk, a torch, a mirror. Leader relates these to qualities of the Bible, God's gift to us.*	1,2,3,4
☌ ✋ ☺	⧗ ✉	RHYME FOR YOUNG CHILDREN. (CFAA p. 218) Jesus I am loved by you	1,2,(3,4)
		AFFIRMATION OF FAITH (PFW p. 61, 6F7)	3,4

Thread 3	Thread 4	**THE CONCLUSION** Thread 2	Age-group
👆✋ ☺	⏳ ✉	KYRIE CONFESSION (PFW p. 48) *Requires two leaders.*	(2),3,4
		ABSOLUTION	1,2,3,4
👆✋ ☺	⏳ ✉	INTERCESSIONS (CFAA p. 218)	(2),3,4
☺	✉	The Lord's Prayer	(1),2,3,4
		SONG (CFW 621) Thanks to God whose word	(1,2),3,4
👂✋☺✠	⏳✉✈	*Congregation goes forward to collect their Bibles.*	1,2,3,4
		PRAYER	
		SONG (JP 228) Tell me the stories of Jesus	(2),3,4
👂✠		BLESSING	1,2,3,4

PREPARATION AND RESOURCES

Before the service, ask members of the congregation to bring a Bible that has some personal significance to them. Enough Bible portions should be prepared with important texts (e.g. John 3.16) to give to all those who do not bring a Bible with them, so that everybody can come forward and place something on the display and collect it afterwards.

Prayer of thanksgiving (CFW 618)

The four words 'Thanks be to God' should each be written on one of four large Bible-shaped cards on spare sticks and held up by children each time the response is to be said. The final response, 'To you, O gracious Father', is held up at the end.

Leader For the majesty of the Law, for the power of the Prophets, for the wisdom of the Proverbs and the beauty of the Psalms, and above all for the grace of the Gospel, we lift up our hearts in praise.

All **Thanks be to God!**

Leader For the Bible in our own language, for those who long ago gave us translations, for those who down the years improved them, enabling the Scriptures to penetrate deeply into our national life, we lift up our hearts in praise:

All **Thanks be to God!**

Leader For the continuing work of revision to match our changing language, for all that the Bible means to Christians throughout the world, we lift up our hearts in praise:

All **Thanks be to God!**

Leader For those who interpret, publish and distribute the Scriptures in every tongue, so that all peoples may come to the knowledge of salvation, we lift up our hearts in praise.

All **Thanks be to God.**

All **To you, O gracious Father, with the living Word, through the one eternal Spirit, be glory now and for ever. Amen.**

Rhyme for young children (CFAA p.218)

Jesus, I am loved by you *(hands crossed over chest),*
The Bible tells me this is true *(hands open side by side as if reading a book).*
Help me turn away from wrong *(turn from left to right),*
Let me please you all day long *(hands in the air).*

Affirmation of faith (PFW p. 61, 6F7, after CFW 256)

Let us declare our faith in the resurrection of our Lord Jesus Christ:
Christ died for our sins
in accordance with the scriptures;
he was buried;
he was raised to life on the third day
in accordance with the scriptures;
afterwards he appeared to his followers,
and to all the apostles:
this we have received,
and this we believe. Amen.

Kyrie confession and absolution (based on Psalm 119.1, 2, 5, 6; see PFW p. 48)

Leader 1   God tells us that we will be blessed if we follow his Word; but because we fail to do this we need to confess our sins, saying/singing 'Lord have mercy, Christ have mercy, Lord have mercy'.

Leader 1   Blessed are those whose way is blameless.
Leader 2   But we do not walk in the law of the Lord.
All   **Lord have mercy.**

Leader 1   Blessed are those who keep his command.
Leader 2   But we do not seek him with our whole heart.
All   **Christ have mercy.**

Leader 1   If only our ways were unerring towards the keeping of your statutes.
Leader 2   But we are ashamed when we look on all your commandments.
All   **Lord have mercy.**

Intercessions (CFAA p. 218)

Lord God, we pray for all those who use the Bible to teach and preach. Help them to be thorough, but not boring. Long ago you gave us the Bible,
May it challenge and change us today.

For scholars who study the Bible in the light of twentieth century knowledge. Help them to be open-minded, but not unbelieving. Long ago you gave us the Bible,
May it challenge and change us today.

For those who translate the Bible into new languages. Help them to be accurate, but always relevant. Long ago you gave us the Bible,
May it challenge and change us today.

For all who hear the Christmas readings this month. May they sound comforting and familiar, yet be full of new insights. Long ago you gave us the Bible,
May it challenge and change us today.

Prayer

All   **We commit ourselves not to take our Bible for granted, but remembering the message of God's love it contains: to treasure it, to read it, to live it and to share it. In the name of Jesus, the living Word. Amen.**

All-age service for Epiphany

Thread 3	Thread 4	THE PREPARATION Thread 2	Age-group
☺	⌛	GREETING AND SENTENCE Matthew 2.11	3,4
☺	⌛ ✉	PREPARING TO PRAISE (CFAA p. 170)	2,3,4
		COLLECT FOR PURITY (ASB p.119 para.3)	(1,2),3,4
☺	✉	THE LORD'S PRAYER	(1),2,3,4
		THE MINISTRY OF THE WORD AND PRAYERS	
✋ ᕙ ✋	⌛ ✉	READING Matthew 2.1–12	
✸ ☺ ✠	✈	*Before reader starts to read, children dressed as Mary and Joseph come and sit by the 'star'.*	
		Following the reading of the Bible story, the children re-enact the story using the 'Wise Men' track in the Nativity play tape, Music 'n' Mime Scripture Press.	(1),2,3,4 1,2,3,4
☺		SONG (JP 271) We three kings	3,4
✠	⌛	SHORT ADDRESS 'Led by a star'	3,4
		THE PRAYERS	
☺		PRAYER OF CONFESSION For Epiphany (CFW 94)	(2),3,4
		ABSOLUTION	1,2,3,4
		SONG (JP 253) The wise may bring their learning	(2),3,4
✋ ᕙ ✋ ☺ ✠	⌛ ✉ ✈	*During this song children give out cardboard stars to the congregation. Each point of the star has one item of intercession printed: Church, world, local community, sick, bereaved. On the reverse of the star is printed the Epiphany Collect.*	1,2,3,4
ᕙ ✋	✉	INTERCESSIONS	(2),3,4
		COLLECT for Epiphany (ASB p. 460)	3,4
		THE CONCLUSION	
		SONG (JP 9) As with gladness men of old	3,4
ᕙ ✠		BLESSING	1,2,3,4

80

PREPARATION

Have two children dressed as Mary and Joseph carrying a suitably dressed doll, and have three children dressed as Wise Men carrying gifts. Erect a star above the place where Mary and Joseph will stand. Find the appropriate track on the *Music 'n' Mime* tape and arrange suitable amplification. Make cardboard stars for each member of the congregation, approximately 5cms in diameter, as described in the order of service.

RESOURCES

Greeting and sentence

> The Lord be with you
> **and also with you.**

Leader   On coming to the house, the wise men saw the child, and his mother Mary, and they bowed down and worshipped him (Matthew 2.11).

Preparing to praise (CFAA p. 170)

God has called us here this morning,
All the world give God your praises,
Let us offer him our worship,
All the world give God your praises,
Let us thank him for his goodness,
All the world give God your praises,
Let us ask him to forgive us,
All the world give God your praises,
Let us learn what he would teach us,
All the world give God your praises,
Let us bring our prayers before him,
All the world give God your praises.

Confession and absolution *(CFW 94)*

Lord Jesus Christ, wise men from the East worshipped and adored you; they brought you gifts – gold, incense, and myrrh.

We too have seen your glory, but we have often turned away. Lord, in your mercy,
forgive us and help us.

We too have gifts, but we have not fully used them or offered them to you. Lord, in your mercy,
forgive us and help us.

We too have acclaimed you as King, but we have not served you with all our strength. Lord, in your mercy,
forgive us and help us.

We too have acknowledged you as God, but we have not desired holiness. Lord, in your mercy,
forgive us and help us.

We too have welcomed you as Saviour, but we have failed to tell others of your grace. Lord, in your mercy,
forgive us and help us.

Make our trust more certain,
make our love more real,
make our worship more acceptable,
for your glory's sake. Amen.

All-age service for the Ninth Sunday Before Easter

Theme: *Jesus the teacher*

Thread 3	Thread 4	THE PREPARATION Thread 2	Age-group
☙ ✠		**GREETING**	1,2,3,4
		Leader Today we are thinking about the teaching of Jesus, and the way Jesus' teaching challenged the teaching of the day by turning it on its head. Let us think of some of those things as we stand and sing.	
♫	✉	SONG (LP 148) O Lord, all the world belongs to you	(2),3,4
		At the last line of each verse have a banner held up with the words 'Turning the world upside down' (keep the banner held up during prayers).	3,4
		COLLECT FOR PURITY (ASB p. 119)	(1,2),3,4
		COLLECT FOR THE DAY (ASB p. 486)	3,4
		THE MINISTRY OF THE WORD AND PRAYERS	
☙ ♫ ☺	⌛ ✈ ✉	INTRODUCTION	(1),2,3,4
		Leader Already in the service you have seen and heard the words 'upside down'. Some of the children are going to show us some things that look different when they are upside down. *(e.g. Beavers showed how they stood on their heads. Guides did a short sketch of people's attitudes being turned upside down. Brownies showed 'upside-down' dolls they had made.)*	
☙ ♫		*Leader* This shows us things are not always what they seem to be. By turning them upside down they are changed. Now we are going to sing another song.	(2),3,4
		The next song is held up on a board or is projected on the OH upside down.	

🕯 ✍ ☺	⏳ ✈	*Leader* Who can work out what we're supposed to sing? Let's now have it the right way round, and sing it with the actions. It's a song about how God has changed a lot of things. SONG (JP 60) God's not dead	(2),3,4
☺	⏳ ✉	*Leader* Now let's listen to a reading that is all about Jesus taking hold of things and turning them upside down. READING Matthew 5. 1–12 *(This could be from the Dramatised Bible.)* *Leader* We now sing about some of those words of Jesus. SONG (A&M 335) Blest are the pure in heart	3,4 (1),2,3,4
🕯 ✍ ☺ ✠	⏳ ✉	*Leader asks four children to come forward, each with a banner with a ☹ on one side and ☺ on the other. As the leader retells each of the first four beatitudes in simple words, one of the banners is turned from ☹ to ☺ .* SONG (CMP 170) Give thanks with a grateful heart	 (1),2,3,4
🕯 ✍ ✋ ☺ ✉ ⏳ ✈ ✠		*Leader then distributes badges with a ☺ that can be turned round from 'sad' to 'happy'. The leader similarly retells the other four beatitudes, and the people turn their badges round. There should be a big badge on the OHP or on a board to demonstrate this.*	
🕯 ☺	✉ ⏳	AFFIRMATION OF FAITH (PFW p. 58, 0F2)	(1),2,3,4
		THE PRAYERS	
🕯 ☺	✉ ⏳	PRAYER OF CONFESSION for our wrong values (PFW p. 44, 0C10) ABSOLUTION	2,3,4
🕯 ☺	✉ ⏳	PRAYER FOR STRENGTH to follow Jesus (CFW 150) with response on OH or board: **'help us to follow'**.	(1),2,3,4

		SONG (CMP 456) Make me a channel of your peace	3,4
		REFLECTION *Have the congregation read the song slowly, giving time to ask God to give us his peace and to make us channels of it to others.*	3,4
		INTERCESSIONS *Link with the words of St Francis: e.g. after the words 'where there is hatred, let me sow love' pray for all who feel hated and neglected by the world, and for the love of Jesus to reach them.*	(1),2,3,4
☺	✉	The Lord's Prayer	(1),2,3,4
		THE CONCLUSION	
		SONG (LP 133) Love is his word	3,4
✿ ✠		BLESSING	1,2,3,4

RESOURCES

Affirmation of faith (PFW p. 58, 0F2)

Jesus calls us to trust, even when our world is turned upside down. Let us then declare that 'we believe and trust in him'.

Do you believe and trust in God the Father,
who made all things?
We believe and trust in him.

Do you believe and trust in his Son Jesus Christ,
who redeemed the world?
We believe and trust in him.

Do you believe and trust in his Holy Spirit,
who gives life to the people of God?
We believe and trust in him.

This is the faith of the Church.
This is our faith.
We believe and trust in one God,
Father, Son and Holy Spirit. Amen.

Confession and absolution (PFW p. 44, 0C10, after CFW no.135, by Michael Perry)

God our Father,
we come to you in sorrow for
our sins.

For turning away from you,
and ignoring your will for our lives;
Father, forgive us:
save us and help us.

For behaving just as we wish,
without thinking of you;
Father, forgive us:
save us and help us.

For failing you by what we do,
and think and say;
Father, forgive us:
save us and help us.

For letting ourselves be drawn away from you
by temptations in the world about us;
Father, forgive us:
save us and help us.

For living as if we were ashamed
to belong to your Son;
Father, forgive us:
save us and help us.

Prayer for strength to follow Jesus (CFW 150)

Jesus said: 'If one of you wants to be great, he must be the servant of the rest'.
Master, we hear your call:
help us to follow.

Jesus said: 'Unless you change and become humble like little children, you can never enter the Kingdom of heaven'.
Master, we hear your call:
help us to follow.

Jesus said: 'Happy are those who are humble; they will receive what God has promised'.
Master, we hear your call:
help us to follow.

Jesus said: 'Be merciful just as your Father is merciful; love your enemies and do good to them'.
Master, we hear your call:
help us to follow.

Jesus said: 'Love one another, just as I love you; the greatest love a person can have for his friends is to give his life for them'.
Master, we hear your call:
help us to follow.

Jesus said: 'Go to all peoples everywhere and make them my disciples, and I will be with you always, to the end of the world'.
Master, we hear your call:
help us to follow.

**Lord, you have redeemed us
and called us to your service:
give us grace to hear your word
and to obey your commandment;
for your mercy's sake. Amen.**

All-age service for Mothering Sunday

Thread 3	Thread 4	THE PREPARATION Thread 2	Age-group
☺	⧖	GREETING	(2),3,4
		INTRODUCTION	2,3,4
		Leader Today is a special day. It is Mothering Sunday – not Mother's Day – that is something quite different which the Americans celebrate on the second Sunday in May, but it has no particular religious significance. Mothering Sunday has its roots in the traditions of the Church, going back for hundreds of years.	
		Back in the Middle Ages parishes covered a very wide area and often had both a parish church and a lot of daughter churches (known as Chapels of Ease). Week by week parishioners worshipped in their little local churches, but halfway through Lent, on the Fourth or Mid-Lent Sunday, everyone was required to attend a service at the main parish church. Groups would meet up and walk in procession from the outlying villages and hamlets to their Mother Church. Those who had left home to work would also find their way back and there would be great family reunions. We think of those processions now as we sing.	
✋ 🖐 ☺ ✠	⧖ ✉ ✈	SONG (A&M 629) Onward Christian soldiers *(during which children bring placards to the front with names of local chapels of ease).*	1,2,3,4
	⧖	PRAYERS (PFW p. 36, 0A21)	(2),3,4
		COLLECT for Christmas 2, Year 1 (ASB p. 455)	
✋ ☺	⧖ ✉	SONG (JP 21) Brothers and sisters *(congregation repeat each line)*	1,2,3,4

Thread 3	Thread 4	**THE MINISTRY OF THE WORD** Thread 2	Age-group
✋ 𝄞 ☺ ✠	⧗ ✉	ADDRESS 1 Mother Church in the past *Highlight map of your locality to show chapels of ease. It will then be simpler to put up a simplified sketch or map of your area and then add the captions:* 1. **Giving birth:** she gave birth to them – without her they could not have come into being. 2. **Feeding:** she fed them – offering nourishment and sustenance – first milk and then solids. 3. **Comforting:** she comforted them – in dispute and squabble, in sadness and distress. 4. **Teaching:** she taught them – from her own wisdom and experience. 5. **Suffering:** she suffered – when they rebelled and pulled in other directions.	(1),2,3,4
		READINGS About gathering to worship God. Psalm 100 Come and worship Luke 13. 34 –35 Jesus longs to gather the people.	3,4
✋ 𝄞 ☺ ✠	⧗ ✉	ADDRESS 2 Mother Church today *Put the five captions ('Giving birth' etc.) on OH or board, then put in a picture of your local church(es). Point out that the Church today does the same things for the people of the parish. This is not just the work of one person (the priest), but what we all do for one another.*	(1),2,3,4
✋ 𝄞 ✋ ☺	⧗ ✉ ✈	SONG (JP 367) I am the Church, you are the Church (with actions)	1,2,3,4
☺ ✠	⧗	AFFIRMATION OF FAITH (PFW p.62, 0F9)	(2),3,4

Thread 3	Thread 4	**THE PRAYERS** Thread 2	Age-group
		Leader Of course we know that all too often we fail to care for one another in this way. So let us now tell God how sorry we are.	(2),3,4
☺	⌛ ✉	PRAYER OF CONFESSION (PFW p. 44, 0C10)	(2),3,4
		ABSOLUTION	1,2,3,4
☺	⌛	OFFERTORY SONG (JP 254) Think of a world	(2),3,4
☺	✉	INTERCESSIONS The Lord's Prayer	(1), 2,3,4
		THE CONCLUSION	
🕯 ᔐ ☺	⌛ ✉	ADDRESS 3 Our mothers today *Put up OH of captions but replace picture of local churches with picture of a mother and her child.*	1,2,3,4
🕯 ☺	⌛ ✉	PRAYER OF THANKSGIVING	(1),2,3,4
✠	⌛ ✉ ✈	BLESSING AND DISTRIBUTION OF FLOWERS	1,2,3,4
ᔐ ✠		BLESSING OF CONGREGATION	1,2,3,4
☺		SONG (A&M 171) For the beauty of the earth	(1,2),3,4
☺		DISMISSAL	1,2,3,4

PREPARATION

Have ready a large local map, or prepare an overhead of your local map, so that children can point out the places when you name the ancient 'Chapels of Ease'. Prepare either an OH or large chart with a simplified map of your area with the ancient Mother Church in the centre, and the Chapels of Ease grouped around. The one produced for our area looked like this:

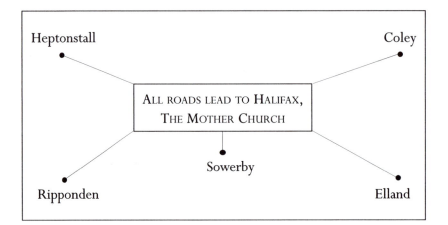

Heptonstall

Coley

ALL ROADS LEAD TO HALIFAX,
THE MOTHER CHURCH

Sowerby

Ripponden

Elland

Make cards or OHs with the captions:

GIVING BIRTH

FEEDING

COMFORTING

TEACHING

SUFFERING

They can then fit on to the chart of the local churches, and be used to teach about Mother Church today.

Have a picture of a mother and child to place above the five captions to relate those qualities to those of a mother in her family.

RESOURCES

Greeting

> The Lord is here.
> **His Spirit is with us.**

Prayers (PFW p.36, 0A21)

**Loving Lord, fill us with your life-giving,
joy-giving, peace-giving presence, that we
may praise you now with our lips and all
the day long with our lives, through Jesus
Christ our Lord. Amen.**

Affirmation of faith (PFW p. 62, from CFW 192 0F9)

**We believe in God the Father,
from whom every family
in heaven and on earth is named.
We believe in God the Son,
who lives in our hearts through faith,
and fills us with his love.**

**We believe in God the Holy Spirit,
who strengthens us
with power from on high.**

**We believe in one God;
Father, Son and Holy Spirit. Amen.**

Prayer of confession and absolution (PFW p. 44, from CFW 135 0C10)

God our Father,
we come to you in sorrow for
our sins.

For turning away from you,
and ignoring your will for our lives;
Father, forgive us:
save us and help us.

For behaving just as we wish,
without thinking of you;
Father, forgive us:
save us and help us.

For failing you by what we do,
and think and say;
Father, forgive us:
save us and help us.

For letting ourselves be drawn away from you
by temptations in the world about us;
Father, forgive us:
save us and help us.

For living as if we were ashamed
to belong to your Son;
Father, forgive us:
save us and help us.

Offertory song (First three verses in JP 254)

4.   Think of a world without any worship,
        Think of a God without his only Son.
        Think of a cross without a resurrection,
        Only a grave and not a victory won:
        We thank you, Lord, for showing us our Saviour,
        We thank you, Lord, and praise your holy name.

5.   Thanks to our Lord for being here among us,
        Thanks be to him for sharing all we do.
        Thanks for our church and all the love we find here,
        Thanks for this place and all its promise true:
        We thank you, Lord, for life in all its richness,
        We thank you, Lord, and praise your holy name.

Prayer of thanksgiving

The qualities of Mother Church are the qualities of mothers and carers for whom we give thanks today. So let us pray and give thanks:

For our mothers who gave us birth:
thank you, Father God.

For our mothers who fed and nourished us:
thank you, Father God.

For our mothers who comforted us when we were sad:
thank you, Father God.

For our mothers who taught us how to live:
thank you, Father God.

For our mothers who suffered when we went astray:
thank you, Father God.

All-age service for Easter Day

Thread 3	Thread 4	THE PREPARATION Thread 2	Age-group
✋〰☺✠	⌛✉	LIGHTING OF EASTER CANDLE	1,2,3,4
		ENTRANCE SONG (A&M 134) Jesus Christ is risen today	
✋ ☺	✉✈	*N.B. repetition of Alleluias. Small children should wave their 'Alleluia' flags as each Alleluia is sung.*	
		COLLECT FOR EASTER DAY (ASB p. 595)	3,4
	⌛✉	GREETING	
✋	⌛✉✈	*Small children should wave their 'Alleluia' flags.*	1,2,3,4
		THE MINISTRY OF THE WORD	
		READING John 20.1–18 (ASB p. 578)	3,4
✋〰☺✠	⌛✉✈	ADDRESS 1: Footsteps 1	1,2,3,4
		Children are asked to make four 'journeys' to and from the Easter Garden along trails of paper footprints on the floor.	
		a) Mary Magdalen to the tomb: feeling sad, she finds the tomb empty.	
		b) Disciples run from the tomb, puzzled.	
		c) Disciples run to the tomb, hopeful.	
		d) Mary Magdalen and the men run from the tomb: the men, still puzzled; Mary Magdalen glad.	
✋〰✋☺	⌛✉	PRAISE SONG Thank you, Lord, for Easter Day	1,2,3,4
		Small children should wave their 'Alleluia' flags as each Alleluia is sung.	
✋〰☺✠	⌛✉	ADDRESS 2: Footsteps 2	1,2,3,4
		Tell the story of the Road to Emmaus.	
✋〰☺✠	⌛✉	SONG (JP 365) Hosanna, hosanna	(1),2,3,4

🕯 〰 ✠	⏳ ✉	**ADDRESS 3: Footsteps 3**	1,2,3,4
		The dream — use the well-known story of the man walking by the sea-shore and seeing his life as two sets of footprints. Conclude with the promise of Jesus: 'I am with you always.'	
☺	✉	CONFESSION (PFW p. 41, 6C4)	(1,2),3,4
		ABSOLUTION	1,2,3,4
🕯 ☺		SONG (JP 320) Children, join the celebration	
〰 ✋ ✹ ☺ ✠	⏳ ✉ ✈	**RENEWAL OF BAPTISMAL PROMISES AND AFFIRMATION OF FAITH** (ASB pp. 276–7 paras 96–8)	1,2,3,4
		After the promises, the light is passed from the Easter Candle and from hand-candle to hand-candle round the church.	
		THE PRAYERS	
🕯 〰 ✋ ☺ ✠	✉ ✈	OFFERTORY SONG (JP 3) Alleluia, alleluia, give thanks to the risen Lord	1,2,3,4
		Children wave 'Alleluia' flags during chorus.	
☺		INTERCESSIONS AND THANKSGIVING	3,4
☺	✉	THE LORD'S PRAYER	(1),2,3,4
		THE CONCLUSION	
☺		SONG (CMP 689) Thine be the glory	(2),3,4
〰 ✠		BLESSING	1,2,3,4

PREPARATION

- Make flags for all the children with 'Alleluia' and suitable designs.

- Ensure the Easter (Paschal) Candle and Easter Garden are ready.

- Cut out paper footprints and lay tracks from the body of the church to and from the tomb in the Easter Garden. (During the service, for the 'Emmaus' and 'Dream' stories, turn one set of tracks round so they both go the same way, *from* the tomb. For the 'Dream' story some of the footprints in one of the tracks will have to be removed for the times when the traveller thought he was alone.)

RESOURCES

Greeting

Alleluia! Christ is risen.
He is risen indeed. Alleluia!

Praise song Thank you, Lord, for Easter Day (tune 'Skip to my Lou')

1. Thank you, Lord, for Easter Day (x3)
   Jesus Christ is risen!

2. Thank you, Lord, you've risen again (x3)
   Jesus Christ is risen!

3. Thank you, Lord, you live today (x3)
   Jesus Christ is risen!

4. Thank you, Lord, we live in you (x3)
   Jesus Christ is risen!

5. Thank you, Lord, you live in us (x3)
   Jesus Christ is risen!

6. Thank you, Lord, you're Lord and King (x3)
   Jesus Christ is risen!

Confession and absolution (PFW p. 41, Easter Confession 6C4 from CFW 244)

O Jesus Christ, risen master and triumphant Lord,
we come to you in sorrow for our sins,
and confess to you our weakness and unbelief.

We have lived by our own strength,
and not by the power of your resurrection.
In your mercy, forgive us.
Lord, hear us and help us.

We have lived by the light of our own eyes,
as faithless and not believing.
In your mercy, forgive us.
Lord, hear us and help us.

We have lived for this world alone,
and doubted our home in heaven.
In your mercy, forgive us.
Lord, hear us and help us.

Renewal of baptismal promises (ASB p. 276 para. 96)

Do you turn to Christ?
Answer   **I turn to Christ.**

Do you repent of your sins?
Answer   **I repent of my sins.**

Do you renounce evil?
Answer   **I renounce evil.**

Affirmation of faith (ASB p. 277 paras 97–8)

Do you believe and trust in God the Father, who made the world?

Answer **I believe and trust in him.**

Do you believe and trust in his Son Jesus Christ, who redeemed mankind?

Answer **I believe and trust in him.**

Do you believe and trust in his Holy Spirit, who gives life to the people of God?

Answer **I believe and trust in him.**

This is the faith of the Church.

All **This is our faith.**
We believe and trust in one God,
Father, Son, and Holy Spirit.

All-age service for the Fourth Sunday after Easter

Theme: *Way, Truth and Life*

Thread 3	Thread 4	**THE PREPARATION** Thread 2	Age-group
💧 ☺	⌛ ✉	SONG (JP 65) Go, tell it on the mountain	2,3,4
		GREETING	(2),3,4
		COLLECT FOR PURITY (ASB p. 119 para.3)	(1,2),3,4
		COLLECT FOR THE DAY Easter 4 (ASB p. 617)	3,4
		THE MINISTRY OF THE WORD	
💧 🐟 ✋ ☺	⌛ ✉ ✈	READING Proverbs 4. 10–19	3,4
		Leader — after the reading, have a tray with seven objects: bread, light bulb, gate, sheep, obituary column, grapes, map. Get children to try to memorise, and then to find seven envelopes hidden around the church with seven 'I am' sayings: 'I am the Bread of Life', 'I am the Light of the World', 'I am the Gate', 'I am the Good Shepherd', 'I am the Resurrection and the Life', 'I am the Vine', 'I am the Way, the Truth, and the Life'. Get children to match them. Then ask them to recognise which one is in the Gospel for the day:	1,2,3,4
		GOSPEL John 14.1–11 (ASB p. 621)	3,4
		SONG (JP 89) 'I am the Way, the Truth and the Life', That's what Jesus said	(2),3,4
💧 🐟 ✋ ✠ ☺	⌛ ✉	*Leader — have compass, map, flask of water ready. Compare compass to the Way, map to the Truth, water to the Life.*	1,2,3,4
☺		SONG (JP 98) I have decided to follow Jesus	2,3,4
💧 🐟 ✋ ☺ ✠	⌛ ✉ ✈	*Leader — have footprints laid round church in advance, starting at font some going first to lectern, some first to altar. Ask children to trace a trail — from the font as the Way, leading to the lectern for the Truth, and to the altar for the Life.*	1,2,3,4
☺		AFFIRMATION OF FAITH (PFW p.61, 6F7)	2,3,4

Thread 3	Thread 4	**THE PRAYERS** Thread 2	Age-group
☺ ✠		OFFERTORY SONG (JP 188) One more step	(1),2,3,4
☺	⌛ ✉	OFFERTORY PRAYER (ASB p. 129 para. 34)	
☺	⌛ ✉	PRAYER OF CONFESSION (PFW p. 44, 0C10)	
		ABSOLUTION	
☺	⌛ ✉	INTERCESSIONS AND THANKSGIVING	3,4
☺	✉	THE LORD'S PRAYER	(1),2,3,4
		THE CONCLUSION	
☺	✉	SONG (JP 472) The Spirit lives to set us free	2,3,4
✑ ✠		BLESSING	1,2,3,4

PREPARATION

- Before the service, prepare the tray with the seven objects: bread, light bulb, gate, sheep, obituary column, grapes, map. Cover it with a cloth for the memory game.

- Prepare seven envelopes with seven 'I am' sayings: 'I am the Bread of Life', 'I am the Light of the World', 'I am the Gate', 'I am the Good Shepherd', 'I am the Resurrection and the Life', 'I am the Vine', 'I am the Way, the Truth, and the Life', and hide them round the church.

- Lay the trail of footprints from the font, to the lectern, to the altar.

RESOURCES

Greeting

The Lord be with you
and also with you.

Alleluia! Christ is risen.
He is risen indeed. Alleluia!

Affirmation of faith (PFW p.61, 6F7 from CFW 256)

Let us declare our faith in God who has spoken to us through Jesus the Way, the Truth and the Life.

Christ died for our sins
in accordance with the scriptures;
he was buried;
he was raised to life on the third day
in accordance with the scriptures;
afterwards he appeared to his followers,
and to all the apostles:
this we have received,
and this we believe. Amen.

Offertory prayer (ASB p. 129 para. 34)

Yours, Lord, is the greatness, the power,
the glory, the splendour, and the majesty;
for everything in heaven and on earth is yours.
All things come from you,
and of your own do we give you.

Prayer of confession and absolution (PFW p. 44, 0C10, from CFW 135)

God our Father,
we come to you in sorrow for
our sins.

For turning away from you,
and ignoring your will for our lives;
Father, forgive us:
save us and help us.

For behaving just as we wish,
without thinking of you;
Father, forgive us:
save us and help us.

For failing you by what we do,
and think and say;
Father, forgive us:
save us and help us.

For letting ourselves be drawn away from you
by temptations in the world about us;
Father, forgive us:
save us and help us.

For living as if we were ashamed
to belong to your Son;
Father, forgive us:
save us and help us.

All-age service for Petertide

Thread 3	Thread 4	**THE PREPARATION** Thread 2	Age-group
☺	⌛	WELCOME READING The call of Peter, Mark 1.14–20 (ASB p.468)	2,3,4
		THE MINISTRY OF THE WORD AND PRAYERS	
✍ ☩	✉	FISH *An OH or picture of a fish is held up.* *Leader* The symbol of a fish is very important, and has many layers of meaning. But as we look at it now we remember that Jesus' friends were fishermen, and he called them to be fishers of people. Jesus called, they answered. Jesus calls us, and we have answered and come this morning.	2,3,4
☺		SONG (JP 123) I will make you fishers	2,3,4
☺		SONG (JP 47) For I'm building a people	2,3,4
☺		COLLECT FOR PURITY (ASB p.119 para. 3)	(1,2),3,4
		COLLECT FOR ST PETER (ASB p.780)	3,4
♨ ✍ ✹ ☺ ☩	⌛ ✉ ✈	*Children are now asked to look for fish that have previously been hidden, and to bring them and put them in a net.*	1,2,3,4
		SONG (JP 16) Big man	2,3,4
♨ ✍ ☺	⌛	PRAYER A *Have OH ready on screen after song.*	2,3,4
♨ ✍ ☺	⌛ ✉	ROCK AND KEYS *Show a big rock and a bunch of keys. Ask people to listen for 'rock' and 'key' in this reading.*	1,2,3,4
	✉	READING Matthew 16.13–20	3,4
♨	⌛ ✉	*Leader* Peter was learning from being with Jesus who Jesus really was. As he learnt, Peter would become strong and rock-like. Peter would have a key part to play in Jesus' plan. A key thing we can do is to pray. PRAYER B *Have OH ready on screen.*	2,3,4

Symbols	Symbols 2	Content	Ref
👌 🔥 ☺	⧗	*Leader* Because praying is such a key thing, we are going to spend a few moments praying for others.	
		PRAYER B	
👌 🔥 ✹ ☺	⧗ ✉	CLOUD	1,2,3,4
		Produce a cloud — e.g. incense or a shape made from stiff card and held on a stick. Wafting the cloud, tell the Transfiguration story dramatically, emphasising how through the cloud the friends of Jesus caught a glimpse of his true glory.	
	⧗	SONG (JP 160) Majesty	(2),3,4
🔥 ☺	⧗	PRAYER D *Have OH ready on screen.*	2,3,4
👌 ✹ ✠	⧗ ✉	COCKCROW *Play a tape of a cock crowing three times.*	1,2,3,4
	✉	READING Peter betrays Jesus, Mark 14.66–72	3,4
🔥 ✹ ✠	⧗ ✉	*Play cockcrow tape again.*	1,2,3,4
☺		CONFESSION *Have ready immediately after cockcrow.*	(2),3,4
		ABSOLUTION	1,2,3,4
👌 🔥 ✋ ☺	⧗ ✉ ✈	SONGS 1. (JP 291) With Jesus in the boat (*with actions*) 2. (JP 145) Jubilate, everybody (*x4 getting faster with clapped rhythm*)	1,2,3,4
👌 🔥 ☺	⧗ ✉	FISH *Show OH of fish.*	(1),2,3,4
		Leader We've heard the words of forgiveness. Peter heard Jesus forgive him on the beach, when he had gone back to fishing. Jesus told Peter that he still trusted him to be a fisher of men. Peter now obeyed.	
		Let us make our response to Jesus' call as we offer our gifts and praise him.	
✋ ☺ ✠	✈	OFFERTORY HYMN (JP 42) Father, I place into your hands	(2),3,4
👌 🔥 ☺	⧗	PRAYER *Have OH ready on screen immediately after song.*	2,3,4

Thread 3	Thread 4	**THE CONCLUSION** Thread 2	Age-group
✋🐚👋 ☺✠	✉	RECESSIONAL HYMN (CMP 737) We shall stand *During this hymn children give out fish badges to the congregation.* PREPARING TO GO *All turn to face the door.* *Leader* Years later, when Peter really was trying to be a 'fisher of men' he found himself in prison, bound with chains and the door firmly locked. But God took off his chains and opened the door so that Peter could continue this work. We now open our church door, so that we can go out and be fishers of men.	(2),3,4 1,2,3,4
🐚 ☺ ✠	✉ ✈	DISMISSAL	

PREPARATION

You will need:

- Large picture or OH of a fish.

- Enough small fishes for each child, and a net to put them in.

- Big piece of rock and large bunch of keys.

- Incense and thurifer or other means of burning the incense – *or* large cardboard cut-out of a cloud.

- Tape recording of a cock crowing.

- Fish badges for children to give out to congregation. These can be a simple design, photocopied on to a sheet of self-adhesive labels.

RESOURCES

Reading The call of Peter (Mark 1.14–20)

Leader Jesus was walking by the Sea of Galilee when he saw Simon Peter and his brother Andrew on the lake at work with a net, for they were fishermen. Jesus said to them:

All **Come with me, and I will make you fishers of men.**

Leader And at once they left their nets and followed him.

Confession

Lord Jesus, many times we have been like Peter. We have denied you by the things we have thought, by the things we have said, and by the things we have done. We have not followed you. We have failed to learn from you. We have been blind to your glory. You died for Peter, for us, for everyone. You rose again, and are always with us. Please forgive us for your love's sake. Amen.

Absolution

Lord Jesus,
help us to be faithful to you.

Prayers

RESPONSE A

Lord Jesus,
help us to follow you.

RESPONSE B

Lord Jesus,
help us to learn from you.

RESPONSE C

Lord, in your mercy
hear our prayer.

RESPONSE D

Lord Jesus,
help us to see your glory.

Prayer

Jesus said, 'Simon Peter, do you love me?' Peter said:
Lord, you know that I love you.

Jesus said, 'Follow me.'
Lord Jesus, help us to follow you.

Dismissal

Go in peace to love and serve the Lord.
In the name of Christ. Amen.

All-age service for Pentecost 8

Theme: Fruits of the Spirit

Thread 3	Thread 4	**THE PREPARATION** Thread 2	Age-group
☺ 👌 ☺	⧖ ⧖ ✉	GREETING ENTRANCE SONG (JP 255) This is the day COLLECT FOR PURITY (ASB p. 119 para.3)	(2),3,4 (2),3,4 (1,2),3,4
		THE MINISTRY OF THE WORD	
👌 ✍ 🖐 ☺ ✠	⧖ ✉ ✈	*Have leaves and fruits scattered about the church. Have five children each hold a cardboard tree trunk. Get children to match the leaves and fruits with five trees (e.g. horse-chestnut tree with horse-chestnut leaf and with conker).* *Leader* We recognise trees above all by their fruits. How do we recognise Christians? Before we go on to think about that here is a praise song that gives us a hint.	1,2,3,4
👌 ☺	⧖ ✉ ✈	SONG (CFW 472) When the Spirit of the Lord	1,2,3,4
👌 ✍ 🖐	⧖ ✉ ✈	*Leader* So how should we recognise a Christian? Jesus said it was by our fruits, so what sort of fruits? *Ask children to hold captions of spiritual fruits and talk about the nine fruits.* *Leader* But how do these fruits grow in us? Or, put another way, what stops them from growing? *Ask what in nature stops plants from growing. Focus on three causes: (a) poor soil; (b) disease; (c) drought. These are dealt with by (a) plant food; (b) medicine/pruning; (c) water.* *Take one of the cardboard trees, stick on leaf and fruit and demonstrate with plant food, an insecticide spray, a watering can.*	

		Leader The first thing the plant needed was food, and for Christians that food is the teaching that we get from the Bible. So let's get some food now, and hear what the Bible says today. READING Galatians 5 *Leader* We are fed when we tell one another the truths of the Christian faith, so let us declare our faith in God. AFFIRMATION OF FAITH (PFW p. 62, 0F9)	3,4
		THE PRAYERS	
☺ ✠	⧗ ✉	*Leader* Remember that spray used to get rid of the nasty things that stopped the plant growing? All of us have bad things (thoughts, words, deeds) that stop us growing and bearing fruit. We get rid of them, not by spraying ourselves, but by confessing them to God.	(2),3,4
☺	✉	CONFESSION (CFW 465)	(2),3,4
		ABSOLUTION	1,2,3,4
♨	⧗ ✉	*Leader* The third thing that plant needed to be healthy and bear fruit was water. For us that means the refreshment that comes when God's Holy Spirit blesses us. Let us pray for ourselves, and for the world, for that blessing.	(2),3,4
		COLLECT FOR PENTECOST 8 (ASB p. 673)	3,4
☺	⧗	INTERCESSIONS (PFW p.75, 8H12)	3,4
☺	✉	THE LORD'S PRAYER	(1),2,3,4
		THE CONCLUSION	
☺	⧗	OFFERTORY SONG (A&M 205) Love divine	3,4
♨ ☺		OFFERTORY PRAYER (ASB p. 129)	(2),3,4
⚮ ✠		BLESSING	1,2,3,4

111

PREPARATION

● Make five cardboard trees so that children holding them can just look over the top.

● Make labels for five species of tree, and make a leaf and a fruit for each species.

● Make labels of the fruits of the Spirit: love, joy, peace, patience, kindness, goodness, faithfulness, gentleness, self-control.

● Have ready a box or bottle of plant foot, an insecticide spray and a watering can.

RESOURCES

Greeting

The Lord be with you
And also with you.

Affirmation of faith (PFW p. 62, 0F9, from CFW 192)

**We believe in God the Father,
from whom every family
in heaven and on earth is named.**

**We believe in God the Son,
who lives in our hearts through faith,
and fills us with his love.**

**We believe in God the Holy Spirit,
who strengthens us
with power from on high.**

**We believe in one God;
Father, Son and Holy Spirit. Amen.**

Confession and absolution (CFW 465)

O God, we come to you in repentance,
conscious of our sins:

When we are self-satisfied, you expose our failure.
Lord, forgive us:
save us and help us.

When we are self-assertive, you challenge our pride.
Lord, forgive us:
save us and help us.

When we are self-opinionated, you show us we do not know everything.
Lord, forgive us:
save us and help us.

When we are self-indulgent, you condemn our greed.
Lord, forgive us:
save us and help us.

When we are self-centred, you take our peace away.
Lord, forgive us:
save us and help us.

**Give us a new vision of your holiness,
make us worthy to be your people,
and help us to live up to our calling
in Jesus Christ our Lord. Amen.**

Collect for Pentecost 8 (ASB p. 673)

Almighty God,
who sent your Holy Spirit
to be the life and light of your Church:
open our hearts to the riches of his grace,
that we may bring forth the fruit of the Spirit
in love and joy and peace;
through Jesus Christ our Lord.

Intercessions (PFW p. 75, 8H12, from CFW 324)

We pray that God's Holy Spirit may direct our lives [and the lives of others],
saying:
Come to bless us:
and fill us with your Spirit.
'The fruit of the Spirit is
love, joy, peace' –
Father, we know that your world needs love and harmony
[prayers for the Church].

Come to bless us:
and fill us with your Spirit.

'The fruit of the Spirit is
patience, kindness and goodness' –
Father, we know that our world is starved of love and care
[prayers for the sick and bereaved].

Come to bless us:
and fill us with your Spirit.

'The fruit of the Spirit is
faithfulness, gentleness and self-control' –
Father, we know that our world is short of truth and justice
[prayers for the world].

Come to bless us:
and fill us with your Spirit.

**Send us out in his power
to live and work to your praise and glory;
through him to whom we belong,
Jesus Christ our Lord. Amen.**

All-age service for Harvest Festival

Thread 3	Thread 4	**THE PREPARATION** Thread 2	Age-group
🕯☺	⏳	GREETING	3,4
🕯〰✋☀ ☺✠	⏳✉✈	SENTENCE 'The land has yielded its harvest; God, our own God, has blessed us.' HYMN (A&M 482) Come, ye thankful people *During the hymn harvest gifts are brought forward.*	1,2,3,4
🕯☺	✉	PRAYER OF THANKSGIVING	(1),2,3,4
🕯〰	⏳✉	THE MEANING OF THE SUKKAH	1,2,3,4
		Leader You may be wondering why the church is looking as it is today. Let me tell you. In the Bible it says that many years ago Moses and the children of Israel spent 40 years wandering in the wilderness. During that time, as they journeyed to the promised land, God provided them with food and drink. He met their needs. They were never without food and water.	
		Today Jewish people remember God's faithfulness. At harvest time they build temporary shelters, just like the Bible says their ancestors who lived in the wilderness did. We have made the whole church into a shelter (or sukkah).	
		THE MINISTRY OF THE WORD AND PRAYERS	
🕯〰✠	⏳✉	*Leader* Some of you may be wondering what this strange-looking decoration is.	
		READING Leviticus 23. 39–43	(2),3,4
☺✠	✉	*Leader* These shelters remind us that life is a journey – that all the time we are moving on, but as we travel we are reminded that: 'All good gifts around us/Are sent from heaven above/Then thank the Lord,O thank the Lord /For all his love.' Let us sing those words in the	

☺	⏳ ✉	hymn 'We plough the fields and scatter'. We are only going to sing the first two verses but leave your book open so that we can sing verse three later. *Draw attention to the repetitive chorus for children to join in.* HYMN (A&M 483) We plough the fields and scatter (vv. 1 and 2 only)	(1),2,3,4
👆 🐛☺✠	⏳ ✉	THE OPENNESS OF THE SUKKAH *Leader* 'He lights the evening star.' Jewish people make sure that the roof of their hut (sukkah) is made in such a way (usually with leaves and branches) so that you can see through and see the stars in the sky. These are reminders of the One who made them and who protects them in all that they do. All the fruit and vegetables (real and cardboard painted by the children) are a reminder of the way God provides for our needs. It is the children's job to decorate the sukkah and that is why (*give details of children / group / school etc.*) you have been doing just that. As we continue to thank God for his goodness let us sing the third verse of our hymn.	1,2,3,4
👆 🐛	✉	HYMN (A&M 483) We plough the fields (v. 3 only)	2,3,4
👆 🐛✋☺ ✠	⏳ ✉✈	THE LULAV CEREMONY *Leader* Jewish people perform a little ceremony in their sukkah. They have (*invite children out to hold each one*): 1. A palm branch. This is growing straight up in the air. It represents AIR. (*Have you a palm branch left from Palm Sunday?*) 2. A myrtle branch. This grows close to the ground and represents EARTH. (*Improvise a shrub with eye-shaped leaves.*)	1,2,3,4

		3. A willow. This grows by water and represents WATER. 4. An etrog. This is shaped like a lemon and represents a ball of FIRE. *(Use a lemon.)* Everyone shakes these four things together and a blessing is said to thank God for his gifts of earth, air, fire and water.	
👆 ☞ ✋ ☀	⏳ ✉ ✈	**BLESSING A**	1,2,3,4
☺ ✠		*Leader* But as this blessing is offered, the straight palm represents a straight, upright spine, the myrtle leaves represent eyes to read the Word of God, the willow leaves represent lips to praise God, the etrog represents a heart with which to love God. So we have another blessing to say as we shake the lulavs again:	
👆 ☞ ✋ ☀	⏳ ✉ ✈	**BLESSING B**	
☺ ✠		**SONGS**	1,2,3,4
👆 ☞ ☺	⏳ ✉ ✈	1. God's not dead *(N.B. special harvest words)*	
		2. (JP 145) Jubilate, everybody *(clapped rhythm)*	
		3. (JP 78) He's got the whole wide world *(actions)*	
☺	✉	CONFESSION (PFW p.42, 10C6)	2,3,4
		THE CONCLUSION	
		JESUS AT THE FEAST	2,3,4
		We are told in the Bible that Jesus once went to a Harvest Festival. When he did, he took another ceremony, and used it to teach the people about the special gift that he can give.	
		READING John 7. 37–39	2,3,4
		At harvest time we should not just think about the material gifts we enjoy. God wants us to look beyond the gifts to him who is the Giver. And he wants to give us something even more important than these material gifts.	2,3,4

		Jesus promises to give the Holy Spirit to all who are thirsty – to all who need spiritual refreshment and strength. Water is a symbol of the Holy Spirit (we are baptised in water). When we experience a drought we realise more than ever how precious water is. So as we now pour out the water, let us open our hearts to drink in God's gift of his Holy Spirit.	
♨ ↝ ☼ ✠	⧗ ✉	*The water is poured out from the pitcher into the font, and then is said:* BLESSING C	1,2,3,4
♨ ✋ ☺	⧗ ✉ ✈	OFFERTORY HYMN (JP 71) Have you heard the raindrops	1,2,3,4
☺	✉	PRAYERS AND THE LORD'S PRAYER	(1),2,3,4
☺		FINAL HYMN (JP 254) Think of a world *(N.B. The Methodist hymn book has five verses.)*	2,3,4

PREPARATION

As explained in the service, the Jewish Harvest Festival, the Feast of Tabernacles, which we know Jesus attended, involves making a tent (tabernacle – Hebrew word 'sukkah'). Sowerby Church, where this service took place, has a balcony on three sides, so it was decided this year to create the effect of the whole of the ground floor being a 'sukkah'. Strings were stretched across from the north to the south balcony. Ferns and ivy were twisted on to these strings, and cut-out fruits were hung from the strings by cotton. The uniformed groups made these and enjoyed helping to hang them up. About two hundred fruits were needed! The nave altar was used for the sukkah table. However, a large-size model Sukkah within the church could also be used.

By using the story of Jesus at the Feast (John 7) it was hoped to illustrate dramatically the message that God has spiritual as well as material gifts for us.

The baptismal pitcher and a portable font were used for the pouring ceremony. We made one sizeable lulav for the leader, and 100 small ones for the congregation. For the palm we used pieces of palm branch left from Palm Sunday (supplemented by others made of card to make sufficient numbers). We used a lemon for the leader's etrog, and cut-out card lemons for the congregation. Myrtle is not easily available, so we used lilac leaves. Willow herb will do if willow is not available.

Everyone enjoyed waving the lulavs and repeating the blessings. We projected all the prayers, responses and songs from overheads, but books were also available for those who preferred.

RESOURCES

Prayer of thanksgiving

Leader   We thank you, O God

All   **and praise your Holy Name . . . For these and all your blessings we make our harvest thanksgiving and give you all the glory.**

The lulav ceremony

BLESSING A

> **Blessed are you, Lord God, King of all the world; you give for our use the gifts of your creation.**

BLESSING B

> **Blessed are you, Lord God, King of all the world; you made us able to give ourselves in worship and service.**

BLESSING C

> **Blessed are you, Lord God, King of all the world; you pour out your Spirit on all flesh.**

Confession and absolution (PFW p. 42, 10C6, from CFW 511)

We confess our sin, and the sins of our society,
in the misuse of God's creation.

God our Father, we are sorry
for the times when we have used your gifts carelessly,
and acted ungratefully.
Hear our prayer, and in your mercy:
forgive us and help us.

We enjoy the fruits of the harvest,
but sometimes forget that you have given them to us.
Father, in your mercy:
forgive us and help us.

We belong to a people who are full and satisfied,
but ignore the cry of the hungry.
Father, in your mercy:
forgive us and help us.

We are thoughtless,
and do not care enough for the world you have made.
Father, in your mercy:
forgive us and help us.

We store up goods for ourselves alone,
as if there were no God and no heaven.
Father, in your mercy:
forgive us and help us.

Song God's not dead (Adapted from JP 60 using special harvest words which refer to the lulav.)

God's not dead, (no) he is alive. (x3)
Praise him with my lips
See him with my eyes
Love him with my heart
Serve him with my self.

All-age worship with Holy Communion

This service is designed to be led by a priest in the usual way, but with a lay person (designated the 'Leader') commenting on the action and leading the people, including the children, to appreciate and follow what is happening.

BEFORE THE SERVICE

- Lay out a few toys as a bolt-hole for parents who have to take toddlers out of the service.

- Prepare some toddler packs for parents to use with children during the service.

- Arrange people to take part in the mime to accompany the readings.

Thread 3	Thread 4	THE PREPARATION Thread 2	Age-group
		WELCOME	(1,2),3,4
		Leader Welcome to the service this morning. We have come together for the very special service we call Holy Communion, and we are celebrating this service in a way designed to help us think carefully about what it means.	
		There are some toys out in the lounge for small children if parents feel they need to take them out of the service, but we hope you won't have to do that, or if you do that you will come back into church as soon as possible. We have provided some toddler packs, with things in them that can be used at particular points in the service. We will point out when that is most appropriate.	
		However, we can't really just come off the street and be ready to join in this important service. We need some time to prepare ourselves, to recognise that we are here together. So we start our time of preparation by greeting one another, and singing a song.	

☺	⧖	GREETING	(2),3,4
		SONG (CMP 38) As we are gathered, Jesus is here	(2),3,4
		Leader Jesus *is* here, and we want to feel that this is real. So, in familiar words, we ask him to help us to be able to worship.	
		COLLECT FOR PURITY (ASB p. 119 para. 3)	(1,2),3,4
		The leader may suggest that parents give small children their 'sorry' books before the Confession.	
☺		CONFESSION (ASB p. 120 para. 7)	(2),3,4
		ABSOLUTION *(said by priest)*	
		Leader Let us pray that we will learn afresh, or for the first time, something of what this service really means.	3,4
		COLLECT for Thanksgiving for Institution of Holy Communion (ASB p. 920 – *said by priest*)	
		THE MINISTRY OF THE WORD	
		Leader So why do we have this service? To understand this we have to go back to the time right at the end of Jesus' earthly life, when he (and his friends) knew he was going to be killed. Jesus wanted to do something very special for them.	2,3,4
☝☙✋☺✠⧖✉✈		READING Mark 14.12–16	1,2,3,4
		As soon as the reading starts, a man appears carrying a baptism jug. He meets young people carrying table-cloth, candles, chalices and plates. They follow him to the nave altar where he puts the jug down on floor.	
☝	⧖	*Leader* That night Jesus came to this room to have the meal his disciples had prepared. This was the last supper he would have with them. It was at this supper that he gave them a very special way of remembering him, and of them showing they really wanted to be his followers. He promised he would be with them in a special way.	1,2,3,4

♨ ᨆᨆ ♔ ☺ ✠ ⧖ ✉ ✈		READING Mark 14.22–24	(2),3,4
		You can see in that story that Jesus did *four* important things: he *took* bread and wine; he gave *thanks* to God; he *broke* the bread; he *gave* it to his friends.	
		Have four children to hold up placards with these words (and pictures?) on them.	
		We still do what Jesus did that night, and call it Holy Communion.	2,3,4

THE MINISTRY OF THE SACRAMENT

♨ ᨆᨆ ♔ ☺ ✠ ⧖ ✉ ✈		THE PEACE	1,2,3,4
		Priest After he had died on the cross and risen again, Jesus met his disciples on the first Easter Day. And the first thing he did was to have a meal with them, just as he had done at the Last Supper, a few days earlier. We read in the Bible: 'The risen Lord came and stood among friends; he breathed on them the Holy Spirit and said, "As the Father sent me, so I send you. Peace be with you."' So I say to you in his name:	
		Priest Let us offer one another a sign of that peace.	
♨ ᨆᨆ ♔ ☺ ✠ ⧖ ✉ ✈		TAKE	(1),2,3,4
		Leader At the beginning of the service we remembered and enacted how Jesus' disciples made preparations for the meal they were to have with Jesus. Today, followers of Jesus still make preparations for the sharing of the meal which we call Holy Communion, or the Lord's Supper. As we sing the next hymn, you will see people bringing bread and wine to the table for the meal.	
		At the Last Supper Jesus then *took* the bread and wine, and today the priest will *take* the bread and wine ready for the Communion. We believe also that God will *take* the bread and wine and make them into our spiritual food and drink.	

		Christians also feel that the bread and wine are symbols of our daily life. As we bring them to the table we are saying to God:	
		'Here we are: make us into people who will be a blessing to all who meet us.'	
		It seems fitting to make this the point in the service when we can give something to God that he can make use of to help others. So we offer some of our money as well.	
		OFFERTORY SONG (JP 48) For the beauty of the earth *(N.B. repetitive chorus)*	
♨ ᰂ ᰰ ☺ ✠	⧗ ✉ ✈	*The collection is taken, and adults and/or children bring the bread and wine and money to the altar.*	1,2,3,4
♨ ᰂ ᰰ ☀ ☺ ✠	⧗ ✉ ✈	THANK	(1),2,3,4
		Leader The next thing that Jesus did after taking the bread and wine was to say a big thank you prayer. It's like saying grace before the meal. Little children may like to look at their *Thank You* books during this prayer.	
		EUCHARISTIC PRAYER *(led by priest)*	(1,2),3,4
		Before The Lord's Prayer the leader may suggest parents give small children their 'Lord's Prayer' books before saying the prayer.	
☺	✉	THE LORD'S PRAYER	(1),2,3,4
		BREAK	
ᰂ ☀ ✠	⧗	*Priest* We break this bread (ASB p. 142 para. 43)	1,2,3,4
ᰂ ᰰ ☺ ✠	✉ ✈	GIVE	1,2,3,4
		Leader In this parish, people receive the bread and wine at the high altar. People who are not going to receive the bread and wine are warmly invited to come to the altar, with those who are receiving Communion, kneel and bow your head so that we may pray God's blessing on you. Little children may like to hold the brightly coloured shape of a cup and a plate which is in their bags.	

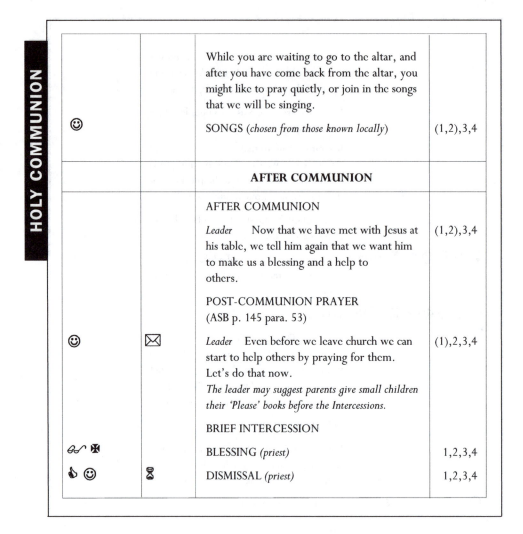

☺		While you are waiting to go to the altar, and after you have come back from the altar, you might like to pray quietly, or join in the songs that we will be singing.	
		SONGS (*chosen from those known locally*)	(1,2),3,4
		AFTER COMMUNION	
☺	✉	AFTER COMMUNION	
		Leader Now that we have met with Jesus at his table, we tell him again that we want him to make us a blessing and a help to others.	(1,2),3,4
		POST-COMMUNION PRAYER (ASB p. 145 para. 53)	
		Leader Even before we leave church we can start to help others by praying for them. Let's do that now. *The leader may suggest parents give small children their 'Please' books before the Intercessions.*	(1),2,3,4
		BRIEF INTERCESSION	
✎ ✠		BLESSING (*priest*)	1,2,3,4
♨ ☺	⧗	DISMISSAL (*priest*)	1,2,3,4

PREPARATION

Toddler packs may contain:

- small board books, e.g. *Please*; *Thank you*; *Sorry* (Candle Books);

- an illustrated book about The Lord's Prayer, e.g. *Little Bible Window Prayers* (Nelson Ward);

- a chalice and pattern shape cut out of foil or holographic card;

- a couple of small soft toys, or a large piece of a jigsaw puzzle, or a matching game.

RESOURCES

Greeting
The Lord be with you
and also with you.

The Peace
The peace of the Lord be always with you
and also with you.

All-age Service of Baptism

As with the all-age presentation of Holy Communion, it is intended that the Baptism Service is led by a priest, but with a commentary spoken by the 'Leader', who is leading the congregation into an understanding of the action. It is also helpful to have a 'Reader' to emphasise some Scripture verses.

Thread 3	Thread 4	THE PREPARATION Thread 2	Age-group
		COLLECT FOR PURITY (ASB p.119 para. 3)	(1,2),3,4
✶ symbols	✶ symbols	*All lights in church switched off.*	(1,2),3,4
		Reader In the beginning God created the heavens and the earth. And God said, let there be light	
		All **and there was light.**	
		Lights switched on.	(2),3,4
✶ symbols		*Leader* Let us sing about the light of that first morning.	
		Song (JP 166) Morning has broken	(1),2,3,4
✶ symbols	✶ symbols	*Procession moves up church, and a server lights candles.*	
		Reader Light has come into the world	
		All **but people loved darkness instead of light.**	
		Main church lights (not chancel) are switched off.	
		THE MINISTRY OF THE WORD	
		Reader The Bible says that people knew God, but they did not give glory to God, and they did not thank him. Their thinking became useless. Their foolish minds were filled with darkness.	3,4
✶ symbols	✶ symbols	*Leader* To symbolise the way humankind turned away from the light of God, let us all turn round and face the back of the church.	(1),2,3,4

	⌛ ✉	*All turn round.* Now, with our backs to the light we are facing into our own shadows. Notice that the little children we are holding are also now facing the darkness. *Reader* The Bible says that God so loved the world that he gave his only son, Jesus, that whoever believes in him, should not perish but have eternal life. Jesus said: 'I am the light of the world: whoever follows me will never walk in darkness but will have the light of life.'	3,4
✐ ☺ ✠	⌛ ✉	*Leader* To symbolise Jesus coming among us, a procession will move down the church with the candle symbolising his light. Please remain facing the back of the church. *Procession moves down to the back of the church, including three people carrying a cross, a Bible and the Easter candle.* *Reader* The Bible says: 'Jesus came proclaiming the Good News of God. The kingdom of God is near. Repent and believe the Good News.'	(1),2,3,4 3,4
✐ ☺ ✠	⌛ ✉	*Leader* Some people turned to Jesus and became his friends. Others turned against him. They nailed him to the cross and he died. *Put out the Easter candle – silent pause.*	(2),3,4
✐ ✠	⌛ ✉	*Leader* But on Easter Day he rose again. *Light Easter candle again.*	(1),2,3,4
☺ ✐ ☺ ✠ ✈		*Leader* Jesus continued to call people to turn back to God and to his light. He calls us today to turn back to him. We take the cross which represents the death of Jesus. We take the candle which represents the life and light of Jesus. And we take the Bible which represents the call of Jesus to follow him. As these are returned to the front of the church, let us turn round so that we face the light. As we turn to the light, we turn our backs on	(1),2,3,4

✋🐦🖐😊 ☒✉✈ ✠	⧖✉	(we renounce) the darkness. As we do that, notice that we are also turning the children we are holding back to the light. *Procession moves back to the front of the church and stands round behind the font. All turn and begin to sing.*	1,2,3,4
		THE BAPTISM AND PRAYERS	
✠		SONG (CMP 652) The light of Christ *(repetitive chorus)*	(2),3,4
		Leader That turning back to the light of God which we see in Jesus is what baptism is all about. So let us put that into words as we say the first of the baptism promises.	3,4
🐦✠	⧖✉	THE DECISION (ASB p. 245 paras 47, 48)	3,4
		Leader We know we can turn to Jesus like this because he died on the cross, and rose again.	3,4
		So we now mark each child who is to be baptised with the sign of the cross. We do this using holy oil, blessed by the bishop, not because there is anything magic in that, but because oil is a sign of God's blessing to us.	
		As the priest makes this mark, members of the congregation might like to make the sign of the cross in the traditional way (*like this*), so that you know that God wants to bless *you*.	
🐦✠	⧖✉	THE SIGN OF THE CROSS (ASB p. 245 para. 49)	(2),3,4
		Leader We have turned back to God. But how can we be sure that he accepts us?	(2),3,4
		Jesus told his friends that when people turn to him and believe in him, then his friends are to baptise those people with water.	
		Reader Jesus said: 'All authority in heaven and on earth has been given to me. Go therefore and make disciples of all nations. Baptise them in the name of the Father and of the Son and of the Holy Spirit. And look, I am with you always, even to the end of the age.'	2,3,4

↝ ☺ ✠	⧖ ✉	*Leader* Now we are ready to move into the baptism. We shall take some water and ask God to bless it.	1,2,3,4
		Priest pours out water into the font.	
		BLESSING OF WATER OF BAPTISM (ASB p. 246 para. 52)	
		AFFIRMATION OF FAITH (ASB pp. 246–7 paras 53–4)	3,4
		Leader So at last we come to the actual baptism.	
		THE BAPTISM (ASB p. 247 para. 55)	
		The priest baptises each child.	
		Leader Now these children really are facing into God's light, so each child is given a lighted candle.	
↝ ✠	⧖ ✉	GIVING OF THE LIGHT (ASB p. 248 para. 57)	1,2,3,4
		Leader To be baptised makes us realise just how special we are in God's sight. We sit and sing.	(2),3,4
		SONG (JP 106) I'm special	
		Leader When we are baptised, we are not alone. We now belong with all the other people who have been baptised, in one big family. That family is called the Church, and that family is now going to welcome the new members.	(2),3,4
🕯↝✋☺✠	⧖✉✈	WELCOME (ASB p. 248 para. 58)	1,2,3,4
		Leader In God's family, turned to God's light, we can experience true peace. And because we are all members together of God's special family, we share that peace together. We join in the ancient custom of offering one another God's peace. Turn to the people next to you, take them by the hand, and be sure to say 'The peace *of the Lord* be with you' – because it is God's peace, not ours, that we are sharing.	3,4
		THE CONCLUSION	
🕯↝✋☺✠	⧖✉✈	THE PEACE (ASB p. 128 para. 30)	1,2,3,4

		Leader We are about to go out into the world now. We are the same people who came into church this morning, but we are also different, because we have turned to God and put our trust in him. As a symbol that we have done that, and that we are going to try to serve him day by day, let us offer our gifts to him as we take the collection. The money we give will be used to help this church spread God's light in this community and beyond.	3,4
		As we offer our gifts we sing.	3,4
🖐 ☺		SONG (A&M 331) O Jesus, I have promised	3,4
☺		OFFERTORY PRAYER (ASB p. 129 para. 34)	3,4
☺		PRAYERS FOR OURSELVES AND OTHERS	3,4
☺	✉	THE LORD'S PRAYER	(1),2,3,4
✍ ✠		BLESSING	1,2,3,4
☺	✉	SONG (JP 472) The Spirit lives to set us free, walk, walk in the light *(N.B. simple repetitive chorus)*	(1),2,3,4
☺		DISMISSAL (ASB p. 145 para. 55)	1,2,3,4

RESOURCES

The decision (ASB p. 245 para. 48)

> Do you turn to Christ?
> **I turn to Christ.**

> Do you repent of your sins?
> **I repent of my sins.**

> Do you renounce evil?
> **I renounce evil.**

The sign of the cross (ASB p. 245 para. 49)

Priest   I sign you with the cross, the sign of Christ.

Do not be ashamed to confess the faith of Christ crucified.

All   **Fight valiantly under the banner of Christ against sin, the world and the devil, and continue his faithful *soldiers* and *servants* to the end of your *lives*.**

Priest   May almighty God deliver you from the powers of darkness, and lead you in the light and obedience of Christ.

All   **Amen.**

The blessing of the water of baptism (ASB p. 246 para. 52)

Priest pours out water into the font.

Priest   Let us pray.

Praise God who made heaven and earth

All   **who keeps his promise for ever.**

Priest   Almighty God, whose Son Jesus Christ was baptised in the River Jordan:
we thank you for the gift of water to cleanse and revive us;
we thank you that through the waters of the Red Sea, you

led your people out of slavery to freedom in the
promised land;

we thank you that through the deep waters of death you
brought your Son, and raised him to new life in triumph.

Bless this water, that your *servants* who *are* to be washed in
it may be made one with Christ in his death and in his
resurrection, to be cleansed and delivered from all sin.

Send your Holy Spirit upon *them* to bring *them* to new
birth in the family of your Church,
and raise *them* with Christ to full and eternal life.

For all might, majesty, authority, and power are Yours, now
and for ever. **Amen.**

Affirmation of faith (ASB pp. 246–7 paras 53–4)

Parents and godparents, you have brought *these children* to
baptism. You must now declare before God and his Church
the Christian faith into which *these children are* to be baptised, and in which you will help *them* to grow. You must
answer for yourselves and for *these children*.

Do you believe and trust in God the Father,
who made the world?

Answer **I believe and trust in him.**

Do you believe and trust in his Son Jesus Christ,
who redeemed mankind?

Answer **I believe and trust in him**.

Do you believe and trust in his Holy Spirit,
who gives life to the people of God?

Answer **I believe and trust in him.**

This is the faith of the Church.

All **This is our faith.**
We believe and trust in one God,
Father, Son and Holy Spirit.

The baptism (ASB p. 247 para.55)

The priest baptises each child:

Priest	N, I baptise you in the name of the Father, and of the Son, and of the Holy Spirit.
Answer	**Amen.**

The giving of the light (ASB p.248 para. 57)

Priest	Receive this light.
	This is to show you have passed from darkness to light.
All	**Shine as a light in the world to the glory of God the Father.**

The welcome (ASB p. 248 para. 58)

Priest	God has received you by baptism into his Church.
All	**We welcome you into the Lord's Family.**
	We are members together of the body of Christ;
	we are children of the same heavenly Father;
	we are inheritors together of the kingdom of God.
	We welcome you.

CHILDREN
AND THE SERVICE OF
HOLY COMMUNION

Ideally, the Service of Holy Communion is the perfect example of all-age worship! It is dramatic, visual and colourful, and yet infinitely profound and mysterious. Most of the criteria we used in Chapter 2 to test an informal Service of the Word for its suitability for children are observable in the liturgy.

♦	= Simplicity	There is a basic simplicity in the structure.
ᵔᶠ	= Visual	Action and colour are of the essence of the service.
✋	= Tactile	The Peace; receiving Communion or a blessing.
✸	= Other senses	Incense and the sound of bells in some churches.
☺	= Participation	Responses, Intercessions, the Peace.
✠	= Symbols being used	Symbolism is basic to the service.
⧗	= Short sections	This is a problem: many spoken parts are very long.
✉	= Reading not necessary	Responses and prayers become familiar.
✈	= Opportunity to move about	The Peace, the Offertory, going to altar rail.

In terms of being genuinely 'all-age', we could say that the tiniest child will appreciate the flicker of candles, and the oldest and most scholarly adult will never plumb all the depths of the service. This is the theory, and we know of parishes where this is also reality.

Particularly impressive is the parish where there is a Monday afternoon 'Family Communion', where the children come running in ahead of their parents after school to join the senior citizens who are already there. Or there is the Urban Priority Area parish, where the full ritual of the Catholic tradition is carried out with a lightness of touch in a congregation gathered in a semi-circle with the crèche children on a rug in the front row.

This is very much in the tradition of the Roman Catholic Church, and of Anglican churches in the Catholic tradition, where children were expected to go to mass, and many adults cherish precious memories of their child-hood experience of mass.

Of course in practice it is not always so positive an experience! Among the problems that cause difficulties are:

●   The 'style' of the worship may be very formal and 'distant'.

●   The Ministry of the Word especially may be too long and tedious for children, because of its wordiness.

●   The exclusion of children from receiving the bread and wine.

Traditionally children in the Church of England cannot be admitted to Holy Communion until they are confirmed, and this often takes place *after* they have left childhood and entered into their teens. This is an enormous source of concern to many people, and a very real stumbling block to the further-ing and developing of the place of children in the Church. We believe that to exclude children in this way is theologically wrong.

In the introduction to this book we discussed the welcome we give to children at baptism. There we declare them to be 'members together of the Body of Christ'. We cannot see how the Church can be justified in denying Holy Communion to any of its members. Nor do we see any merit in the argument that children 'do not understand' Communion. That argument would exclude adults with learning difficulties. Actually it would exclude *everyone*, for who, in the face of all the controversy that has taken place over the centuries about the meaning of Communion, would dare to claim to understand it!

We are very glad therefore that the House of Bishops has issued guidelines (GS 1212) which make very important statements on this whole matter:

> After consultation, every diocesan bishop will have the discretion to make a general policy whether or not to entertain new applications for 'communion before confirmation' to take place in his diocese. If he decides to do so, individual parishes must seek his agreement before introducing it.

Among other stipulations the guidelines urge that 'the incumbent should take care regarding the quality of teaching material, especially that used with children and young people'. Concerning children:

> The priest will ensure that their involvement and preparation is appropriate, and decide how much of this should take place in a separate place. But anyone who is to receive Holy Communion should be present at least for the eucharistic prayer.

We very much welcome these guidelines, and encourage parishes to approach their bishops, and bishops to use positively the discretion they have been given. We are not urging parishes or individuals to break the rules. Rather, this chapter aims to help people to work within the Church *as it is*, and to find ways of making children feel as much a part of the Body of Christ as we possibly can.

In the light of this kind of thinking, many churches would then agree:

- Yes, we do want to be the whole of the Lord's family gathered around the Lord's table for the family meal.

- Yes, we do want to be true to our words in the Baptism Service to welcome children into the family.

- Yes, we do want children to grow up with a very real sense of belonging to the church family, the Body of Christ.

But such firm conviction does *not* mean that all children of all ages are ready for the full diet of the eucharistic liturgy all at once. The practice and experience of many churches has proved this.

We have to ask: *how much* and *which parts* of the eucharistic liturgy are appropriate for children in each age-group?

Children will gain and give a lot from being in the atmosphere of worship and from being in the presence of adult worshippers. But, for most children, this alone is not enough to draw them into a full experience of the service. In many parishes a pattern has developed whereby children go out to classes or a crèche during the Ministry of the Word, and return to the main service either at the Peace, or at the receiving of Communion.

For those parts of the service when children *are* present, we have to ask:

●   How can congregations recognise and welcome a child's contribution?

●   How can children be helped to understand the shape of the liturgy?

●   How can children be helped to participate in different parts of the service as fully as possible, knowing that when it comes to the administration of Communion they cannot receive the bread and wine?

We have tried to answer these questions by suggesting ways of 'opening up' the liturgy to children. We recognise that the President or other ministers are very limited in the ways in which they can engage the attention of children in the action of the service. This is largely because of the physical distance between the ministers and the congregation. A nave altar helps, but in big churches, the distance is still great. Therefore, accompanying adults have to be the worship leaders for the children, and most adults need help with this. How and when do they guide their children?

In addition, there can be different ways of tackling this. For instance:

●   Once a month choose one part of the liturgy and explore that in active and visual ways (confession/creed/intercessions etc.).

●   Once every three months have a special service in which the sermon is dropped and several parts of the liturgy are explored in an active and visual way.

●   Once a year celebrate the Eucharist with a commentary in words and pictures (see Chapter 3). The pictures can be on an overhead projector or they can be in a 'commentary column' on a service sheet.

This is all on the assumption that the parish has, and wishes to keep, its customary way of celebrating Holy Communion. However, there is now another option. Since the publication and authorisation of *Patterns for Worship*, the very flexible Service of the Word can be combined with Holy Communion in the same way as Morning and Evening Prayer. This opens up the additional opportunity of making the whole service, both Word and Sacrament, fully 'all-age' in character.

Parishes that want to explore this option should look at Chapter 2 to help them think about the Service of the Word, and later parts of this chapter to think about the Ministry of the Sacrament itself.

Whether a parish wants to take this more radical approach, or whether it wants to keep the more familiar and traditional pattern of *The Alternative Service Book* throughout, the two sources come together at the Prayers and the Peace, and the Ministry of the Sacrament continues in the same way.

The chart that follows compares these two approaches, that of using the Service of the Word from *Patterns for Worship* with Holy Communion, and that of keeping *The Alternative Service Book 1980* Communion Service intact. The numbers refer to the sections in each book.

In the rest of this chapter we will assume the more traditional approach and take each of the ten sections of the eucharistic liturgy and suggest how they may, on occasions, be opened up in an all-age manner. Additional suggestions are given for those who accompany very young children, or who work with them in a children's corner or crèche area which is part of the service.

The obligatory parts of the service appear in capital letters. The other elements listed are optional. Paragraph numbers from the ASB are indicated in parentheses.

Questions follow each list of suggestions. It is hoped these will be used by parishes to help them grapple with the issues which make so much of what we do inaccessible, not only to children, but to many adults who are newcomers too.

Patterns for Worship		*The Alternative Service Book 1980*	

THE PREPARATION

1	**Greeting**	2	**Greeting**
2	**Penitence** (or in THE PRAYERS)	4–8	Penitence (or later)
3	Hymn, song, or responses	9–10	Kyrie and/or Gloria
4	**The Collect** here or at section 9	11	**Collect**

THE MINISTRY OF THE WORD

5	**Reading(s) from Scripture**	12–15	**Readings**
6	A psalm, or scriptural song	14, 16	Psalm
		17	**Gospel**
7	**A sermon**	18	**Sermon**
8	**Creed** or **Affirmation of Faith**	19	**Creed**

Continue as in ASB

20, 21, 81	**Intercessions**
23–29, 85	**Penitence** (if not earlier)

MINISTRY OF THE SACRAMENT

30–1	**The Peace**
32–5	**Preparation of the Gifts**
36–41	**Eucharistic Prayer**
42–3	**Breaking Bread**
44–9, 77, 86	**Communion**

AFTER COMMUNION

50–6, 77, 86	After Communion
51	**Post-Communion Prayer**
54	Blessing
55	**Dismissal**

The Alternative Service Book 1980

Holy Communion, Rite A

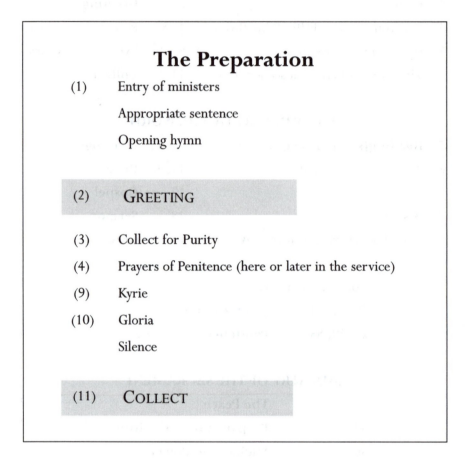

The Preparation

(1) Entry of ministers

Appropriate sentence

Opening hymn

(2) **GREETING**

(3) Collect for Purity

(4) Prayers of Penitence (here or later in the service)

(9) Kyrie

(10) Gloria

Silence

(11) **COLLECT**

In an ideal world we should come to worship well prepared and ready to start, but in reality most people do not. We need a warming-up period – to be ready for communion with God. We need binding together with our neighbours if we are to be the Body of Christ.

When (if) children leave for their groups they can leave in procession taking a Bible with them – showing everyone that they are leaving for their own ministry of the Word.

Hymn

When choosing hymns for parts of the service at which children are present be aware that a lot of children cannot read well enough to cope with hymn books, service papers and overheads.

Choose at least one of the hymns that has a refrain, chorus part or repetition of key word. This can then be announced and children enabled to participate. For example, 'For the beauty of the earth' has the same two-line refrain at the end of each verse, and 'Jesus Christ is risen today' has 'Alleluia' at the end of every line.

Greeting

● On a previous week get everyone to sign a piece of paper suitably cut to make the link of a paper chain. Get a group of children to make the pieces of paper into a massive paper chain – each link being autographed. As the greeting is shared, get a group of children to carry and raise this paper chain. It is explained that as we meet in God's presence we also meet in the presence of one another, joined by his Spirit – like a chain.

● Children make lots of faces on paper plates to which is attached a thread hanger. There must be enough for people in the congregation of all ages to have one each. A large twiggy branch of a tree is mounted at the front of the church. On arrival everybody is invited to 'claim' a face and go and hang it on the tree. At the time of the greeting, people are invited to look at the family tree which symbolises our link to the tree (to God) and to each other. This can help us to realise how in worship we relate to the One who is the source of our life and how we relate to each other.

Collect for Purity

'Cleanse the thoughts of our hearts ....'

● Use the symbol and presence of a large jug and bowl and the pouring of water from the jug into the bowl to illustrate what we are going to ask God to do as we say this prayer.

- Print the prayer on a paper/card on which is drawn either the shape of the jug pouring out water, a tap with running water, or a stream etc. The words can be printed in the space where the water is drawn. Give a card to each child.

- God knows our innermost thoughts and desires. Illustrate this by opening a locked box (or equivalent) and explain that while we can lock things away from each other, we cannot hide anything from God. In this prayer we ask him to cleanse our hidden thoughts and make us able to worship him.

- Give children this beautiful prayer printed on a poster so that they can have it in their bedrooms and learn it by heart.

Kyrie

Because the words of the Kyrie ('Lord have mercy, Christ have mercy, Lord have mercy') are repetitive, they are easy for children to join in. The words can be used with the flavour of both 'Please, Lord' and 'Sorry, Lord', but in either case children need to be told and reminded.

Gloria

Does the setting used for the singing of the Gloria (if any) enable people to feel the Gloria as an expression of praise – a song of joy? There are some versions of the Gloria set to well-known hymn tunes in the book *Five Instant Glorias and a Creed*.

Use liturgical dance to express praise and thanksgiving, thus helping people to see a physical expression of this great song of praise.

Younger children

- Encourage children to watch the procession and look at the colour of the vestments that day. If servers or acolytes carry candles, small children can have their own long 'candles', made from the tubes that come with gift wrapping paper.

- Small children should be encouraged to 'sing' when adults are singing. Give them a book to hold (not necessarily a hymn book), and encourage them to imitate the actions of worshipping adults.

- In the Greeting, make a point of picking up a small child, and with a hug say 'and also with you' or 'and with thy spirit'. The words may not be understood, but the gesture of inclusion most certainly will be.

- Small children could be encouraged to wave praise flags (simple paper flags bearing words of praise to God) during the singing of the Gloria.

Questions about the Preparation

1   In our church how do we use the Preparation for doing just that – preparing people for communication with God?

2   How can the symbolism of the procession and the bringing in of the Book enhance the ministry of the Word?

3   The Preparation is overdone if everything is included. The Greeting and Collect are compulsory. Nothing else is. How do you design the Preparation to best effect?

> for children?
>
> for newcomers?
>
> for long-standing members of the congregation?

When answering Question 3 be aware of the importance of balancing the needs of different groups of people. We cannot meet everybody's needs all the time but it is important that we try to meet everybody's needs some of the time.

Prayers of Penitence

(6) OR (26) AN INVITATION

Time of silence

(7) OR (27) THE CONFESSION

(8) OR (28) THE ABSOLUTION

In the Anglican tradition there is always a prominent place in worship for the confessing of sin.

- We acknowledge that sinfulness is part of the fallen world to which we all belong and that there is need for an expression of confession for the corporate sin of humankind said together.

- We acknowledge the burden of sin which impairs our relationship with God, and our desire to put it right.

There is a choice as to whether the Prayers of Penitence are near the beginning or after the Intercessions. There are good reasons for both positions.

The Prayers of Penitence at the beginning of the service

We cannot come to worship, we cannot relate to our Father in heaven, unless we first put right the relationship that sin has marred. We must heal the relationship before conversation can be restored. We cannot sing God's praises when we have not yet said sorry.

The Prayers of Penitence later in the service after the prayers of Intercession

When we come into church we may have a general sense of sinfulness, and this is a good reason for including the Kyries (Lord, have mercy ...). But, when we have been there for a while, when we have listened attentively to the Scriptures and the sermon and when our prayers have reminded us of the mess our world is in, then we tell God we are sorry. It is the proclamation of the Word that shows us our need for pardon. This links penitence and the Peace – forgiveness and reconciliation (relationship with God and peace with our neighbour).

Confession and Absolution

● Give out tiny pebbles as people come into church. Adults and children are asked to put the pebble in their shoe – it will, of course, be very uncomfortable. There is a lot of symbolism in this which can be used in the developing of the theme. The stone is removed at/after the prayer of confession and pronouncing of absolution. The difference in comfort etc. is quite remarkable.

● Have a vacuum cleaner ready to use. At an appropriate moment tip a lot of fluff and vacuumable rubbish onto the floor. This is particularly effective if your church has a beautifully clean, plain carpet. People are shocked by the mess. Vacuum it up and enjoy the beautiful carpet which has been restored.

● People are invited to write something on slips of paper provided for the purpose. They are asked to identify a burden of sin from which they would like to be free. As they prepare for the confession they take their folded paper and drop it in a metal bin (something like a dustbin). Following the prayer of confession and during the absolution the papers are burned (totally destroyed for ever) in the bin.

Younger children

● Tell children that there is a special moment during the time in church for saying sorry. This can be reinforced by having a small child's book about saying sorry, which can be produced at the appropriate moment, and put way afterwards (in a pocket or handbag) when the 'sorry' time is finished. Good books for this purpose include *Sorry* ('Talking with God' board book) and *I'm Sorry* ('Little Fish' book). Details of these books can be found in Appendix B, p.178.

Questions about the Prayers of Penitence

1. The penitential prayers can come in one of two places in the worship: at the beginning as part of the preparation, or after the Intercessions.

    Discuss the pros and cons of this and decide which you would consider to be the *normal* position of these prayers in your church (see notes).

2. Penitence is always part of our approach to communion. Why?

3. How do we help the following categories of people to seek God's forgiveness?

    children?

    newcomers?

    long-standing members of the congregation?

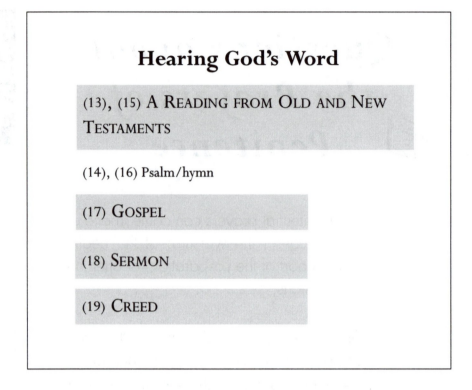

Hearing God's Word

(13), (15) A READING FROM OLD AND NEW TESTAMENTS

(14), (16) Psalm/hymn

(17) GOSPEL

(18) SERMON

(19) CREED

We can approach this part of the service with expectation. Christ is present among his people in the reading of the Scriptures. We have prayed about the theme of the readings in the Collect, and through that prayer we have been opened up to God and to the action of his Spirit. We hear the Scriptures – the Good News.

Reading from Old and New Testaments and Gospel

- A passage of Scripture can be read by one person, or by a group of people reading parts. It can be dramatised or retold in the form of a monologue or dialogue. *The Dramatised Bible* provides scripts for this.

- Mime can stand by itself or be accompanied by a spoken narration, description, poetry or music. Large pictures can illustrate a story, as can banners, posters, stained-glass windows and pictures projected on the overhead.

- The minister (or reader if different) can prepare children for what they are to hear by giving them (immediately before the passage is read) key words to listen for and questions which they can answer after hearing the 'Word'.

- The message that has been heard can be consolidated by using thematic crosswords and puzzles, clipped to a clipboard, for children to complete during the 'adult' sermon.

Sermon

- If children are involved in the sermon, large jig-fit cut words can be hidden round the church for children to find, or they can simply be handed out to children to rearrange in front of the church to form a sentence or phrase from the passage read.

- In the sermon, everyday objects can often be used to focus thinking on a scriptural theme: e.g. salt, glass of water, light bulb, seeds, fruit.

- The 'sermon slot' can be split into two or three shorter spells of time, linked by prayers, hymns, etc. This kind of variety aids concentration.

Creed

- The simpler and shorter Apostles' Creed may be used instead of the Nicene Creed. The ASB also authorises 'The Renewal of Baptismal Vows on Various Occasions'. The three questions and answers from the Baptism Service make it easier for people to grasp the three-fold nature of the credal statement. This also makes a strong link with the Baptism Service for those families who have recently been involved in a baptism. (The Service of the Word allows other forms of Affirmation of Faith to be used on occasion.)

- Make three banners or placards displaying symbols of Father, Son, Holy Spirit. These can be raised at the relevant parts of the Creed giving visual meaning to the words which are spoken. Attach the relevant words from each of the three-fold credal questions and answers to the banner or placard.

Younger children

- Young children may not be able to connect with the passage being read, but they can be trained to know that this is the time in the service when we read from the Bible – God's special book. At this point they can get out their own Bible (e.g. Baby Bible, Toddlers' Bible, Beginners' Bible) or a small Bible story book, to look at the pictures, or just to make the point that this is the time when the Bible is read.

- In some traditions, servers carrying candles stand at the side of the one who reads the Gospel. To children it can be explained that these candles remind us that Jesus is the Light of the World. Small children can make candles in their crèche or playgroup from kitchen roll inner tubes, and they can hold and raise their candles during the reading of the Gospel.

- Very simple activities *which relate to the theme of the day* can be completed during the time of the sermon. These might include sorting, matching, dot-to-dot puzzles, mazes, colouring, etc.

Questions about the Readings, Sermon and Creed

The Scriptures are to be proclaimed and *heard* clearly and joyfully.

What a responsibility for those who come to the lectern! Only a few children are able to read with this kind of fluency and effectiveness. We do not encourage children to read the Scriptures in public unless they can be clearly heard.

1. How do we encourage and train our readers?

2. List as many ways as you can of proclaiming the Scriptures in addition to them being read by a single voice.

3. Think of ways in which children can be involved other than by actually reading the words of Scripture.

4.   What are the implications of these suggestions:

       for children?

       for newcomers?

       for long-standing members of the congregation?

5.   When writing a sermon, how do you decide to what extent children should participate, and to what extent they should be occupied (see Chapter 1)?

6.   The Creed is a statement of faith. When said it can seem long and turgid. Should an affirmation of Christian faith be like that?

7.   How can the Creed be brought to life:

       for children?

       for newcomers?

       long-standing members of the congregation?

Intercessions

(20) INTERCESSIONS AND THANKSGIVING

(21)   Prayers for:
the Church
the world
the local community
those in need
the departed

(23–8) PRAYERS OF PENITENCE
(IF NOT USED EARLIER — SEE p. 142)

(29) PRAYER OF HUMBLE ACCESS

Intercessions are prayers for others. These prayers should be broad so that we offer to God the needs of his whole creation. The question here is not so much about who *leads* the prayers (good as it is for lay people to do this); it is about who *prays* them. These are the *prayers of the people*.

It is important to think about where the one who is praying stands. The prayers must be *heard*. We do not encourage children to lead the Intercessions in public unless they can be heard, and are able to gauge the silences which are basic to this form of prayer.

There are a number of ways of leading Intercessions.

A   1. Leader's material, sometimes extempore, addressed to God.

     2. Silence, for the people to use to make the prayer their own.

     3. A response, 'Lord, in your mercy: hear our prayer'.

     4. A set summing-up paragraph.

B   1. Leader's material.

     2. Silent prayer.

     3. Response.

C   1. Extended bidding prayers followed by set text.

     This method is often used with the Book of Common Prayer, which has a fixed form of Intercessions: the minister gives the congregation a number of prayer intentions or topics, but then reads the prayer (for the whole state of Christ's Church) without interruption.

Intercessions

● Project onto an OH newspaper headlines, pictures, maps etc. concerning the places, situations and people for whom prayers are offered.

● Get children and/or adults to make large placards or banners representing the five sections of the Intercessions (Church/world/community/sick/those who have died). Each picture is made up of helpful symbols and images. The picture is raised as the prayers are offered. Some people (all ages) find it helpful to concentrate on a visual image or symbol as they offer their prayers to God.

● Have a prayer procession. A number of people, well spaced and in good view of all, process around the church carrying symbols, words, objects representative of people, places, etc. People are invited to offer prayers silently for people or places as that symbol/word passes them. Children can make, choose and carry the different things in the procession.

● A method of interceding powerfully and beautifully is used by Roly Bain, a clown and priest. He blows bubbles as a prayer petition is offered. People offer their prayers as the bubbles ascend, and as the bubbles burst silence follows. This can then be repeated for different intercession topics.

● Children can make get-well cards to send/deliver to the people who are sick and who are prayed for by name.

Younger children

● Have a simple jigsaw with seven pieces, five bearing a picture which is a symbol of one section of the Intercessions, one piece with praying hands and the word 'Please', and one piece with the word 'Thank you'.

● Have zig-zag books with one picture page for each section of the Intercessions, a first page saying 'Dear God' and a final page saying 'Thank you'.

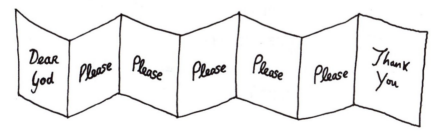

● Use the Candle board book *Please* for this time in the service (see Appendix B, p. 178).

Questions about Intercessions

1. Which of the given styles of interceding feel most like 'the prayers of the people'?

2. Can music be used in intercession? If so, how?

3. 'These are the people's prayers, and the praying probably begins when the reader stops talking' (Michael Perham). What do you feel about this statement?

4. What are the implications for your choice of style of intercession:

    for children?

    for newcomers?

    for long-standing members of the congregation?

The Peace

(30) WORDS AND GREETING

(31) Symbolic action

The Peace acts as a pivot. It makes the transition from Word to Sacrament. The Peace ritualises the command of Jesus to be reconciled to our neighbour before bringing our gifts to the altar. It symbolises:

love and charity between those present at the celebration

the reconciliation of the people in Christ.

The Church is a community. Relationships in that community cannot be taken for granted (as perhaps in the past they could). Relationships need to be made. The Church is about 'community creation' and the greeting of the Peace is a part of that process. What is being affirmed is an amazing thing:

being the Body of Christ

being in love and charity with your neighbour

being reconciled through Christ.

Sharing the Peace

Some churches have reinforced the sense of making one's peace with others and of everyone being united in the Spirit of God by having everyone hold hands round the church and sing a song like 'Peace is flowing like a river'.

Children can be prepared for taking part in the Peace by discussing the words of the Peace in their group and by being given the words of the Peace on a hand-shaped card.

Younger children

Younger children should be encouraged to join in with the sharing of the Peace, and so experience belonging and unity from the earliest possible age.

Questions about the Peace

1. Some people argue for changing the place of the Peace. In so doing it changes its meaning from this pivotal one of reconciliation between Word and Sacrament. What is its meaning:

   at the beginning of the service?

   immediately before the communion (the Roman Catholic position)?

2. How do you make the sharing of the Peace rich in symbolism and meaning instead of it being exclusive or intimidating for:

   children?

   newcomers?

   long-standing members of the congregation?

The Preparation of the Gifts

(32) BREAD AND WINE PLACED ON HOLY TABLE

(33) Prayer of praise to God for his gifts

(34) Offerings of the people

(35) Hymn

This stage of the service is traditionally (and usually) called the Offertory. It moves the service on from Word to Sacrament, and it prepares people for praying the Eucharistic Prayer.

The Offertory is the equivalent of the first of the actions of Christ in the Last Supper. Just as Jesus *took* bread and later *took* the cup, so at the Offertory the priest *takes* the bread and wine and puts them on the altar.

The pattern of action at the Last Supper was that Jesus:

- took bread
- gave thanks
- broke the bread
- took the cup
- gave thanks
- gave it to the disciples.

Because the Church no longer celebrates the Eucharist in the setting of a meal, these actions of Jesus have been combined into four. At the Eucharist the priest:

- takes the bread and the cup
- gives thanks
- breaks the bread
- gives the bread and the cup to the people.

There is a tradition, followed in many churches today, that at the Offertory the priest adds water to the wine. The reason for this custom may be:

- to help prevent possible drunkenness (Justin Martyr);
- to link into John's Gospel account of blood and water flowing from Christ's pierced side;
- to make a link with the water of baptism.

We try to link our worship to our daily life by thinking of the bread and wine as symbols of our human work and experience. God takes them, transforms them and gives them back to us. It was the practice in the early Church for people to bring their own bread and wine to the Eucharist, some of which was used for the celebration, and the remainder went to feed the poor and hungry. A subsequent, but still ancient, development of this practice was for people to give gifts of money or valuables at the same time. When the custom of giving bread and wine lapsed, giving money continued.

Offerings of the people

People must be helped to see that the offering is so much more than the taking of the collection!

- Choose items that are representative of the groups of the church, specific people or projects and form an offertory procession which carries and offers these symbols of their life and work. Children's work can be offered on any or every Sunday as their offering of the use of their developing skills, gifts and talents. We do this kind of offering quite naturally at the Harvest Festival, so why not on other occasions too?

- Help children to identify the four actions, and to realise that this is what Jesus did. You can have a simple card, or four-page picture booklet for the children to use, with your help, at this point in the service.

Younger children

- Encourage younger children to watch and sometimes take part in the offertory procession.
- Encourage them to have money to put in to the collection.

Questions about the Offertory

1. How can we encapsulate the mood of moving from Word to Sacrament? The choice of hymn at this point is important. What should the characteristics of Offertory hymns be?

2. Can you suggest suitable Offertory hymns?

3. How do you grapple with the apparently conflicting ideas that:

   we offer our life and labour to God;

   we come to the Eucharist with nothing?

   'Just as I am, without one plea
   but that thy blood was shed for me.'

4. How do you ensure that this section is neither too short nor too long so that its true function and purpose are conveyed to:

   children?

   newcomers?

   long-standing members of the congregation?

Giving Thanks

(36) TAKING OF THE BREAD AND CUP

(37) THE EUCHARISTIC PRAYER

The word 'Eucharist' means 'thanksgiving', and has become one of the important traditional titles for the service of Holy Communion. This should remind us that:

> giving thanks should be the key-note of the Christian life;

> thankfulness and celebration should be the key-note of this service.

This prayer is meant to be joyful and yet in practice it can seem long and boring, especially to small children. However, there can be quite a lot of participation with the various responses. The Celebrant has the opportunity to make it lively, and command attention. This long prayer is a single prayer, but it falls naturally into three sections, when the Church

* gives thanks for the mighty acts of God;

* recalls the Last Supper and words used during it;

> offers the duty and service of Christian hearts.

The prayer also calls upon the Holy Spirit to make the ritual into reality. However, this remains the most lengthy and difficult part of the service for children and for adults unfamiliar with the service.

Eucharistic Prayer

> Where possible get children gathered around the altar so that they can see what is happening. Do encourage adults to watch too. The drama of the liturgy is powerful.

> Encourage children to learn the various responses and to join in.

> For children's use consider the various children's Communion books (see Appendix B on p.178) that are available.

> Shorter forms of Eucharistic Prayer have been proposed, but these are not yet authorised for use. Some parishes use the shorter ASB 'Eucharistic Prayer for the Sick'.

Younger children

1.   Devise a jigsaw-style activity which simply spells the words 'Thank you'. For very young children the pieces can be matched on to a base board.

2.   The letters could be surrounded by pictures of the things for which we are expressing thanks to God.

3.   Have a simple home-made 'Thank you' book containing pictures stuck in either *by* the child or *for* the child. Pictures which are relevant and attractive to children can be obtained from greetings cards, postcards, crayoning books and catalogues.

4.   Have a 'Thank-you' box. A four-litre ice-cream box lined with felt is ideal for this purpose. Children are given a lot of pictures (creation/life of Jesus, etc.) which they can put one by one into the 'thank-you' box as they say thank you for them.

5.   Use one of the commercially produced 'Thank you' books at this point in the service (see Appendix B, p. 178).

6.   Make a 'Thank you' picture with flaps to lift (as on an Advent Calendar). Under each flap stick a picture of something for which we offer thanks, e.g. Creation, Jesus on the Cross, the Resurrection, etc. Have a border of angels.

Questions about the Eucharistic Prayer

1. How can the 'mystery' of the Sacrament be brought to life for:

    children?

    newcomers?

    adults (who may not be newcomers) who do not receive Communion?

    long-standing communicants?

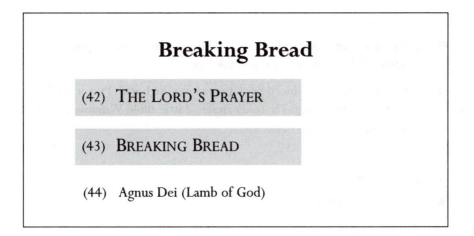

Breaking Bread

(42) THE LORD'S PRAYER

(43) BREAKING BREAD

(44) Agnus Dei (Lamb of God)

Be sure everybody knows which version of the Lord's Prayer is being used. 'Give us this day our daily bread ...' has a special meaning in the eucharistic context. We want children to be totally involved in the praying of this prayer, so activities based upon it may best be done at other times.

Broken bread is very important because it means we *share together* in what Christ has done for us. We can also say that the vocation to follow Christ is about accepting brokenness.

The Lord's Prayer

● Prepare activity sheets for children to use on clipboards, in groups, or at home, based on the words of the Lord's Prayer. Prepare a sheet of the Lord's Prayer with some words missing, and get children to fill in the missing words and illustrate it so that they have made a poster of the words for their bedroom.

● Encourage them to learn this prayer by heart.

● Encourage children to join in with the praying of this prayer.

● Run special series of sermons/talks on the Lord's Prayer. Invite children to illustrate these talks. Display their pictures and posters in the church.

Younger children

- Encourage younger children to learn this prayer and to join in with praying it from the earliest possible age.

- A commercially produced book presenting the Lord's Prayer could be used at this time: e.g. *The Lord's Prayer*, 'Little Bible Window Prayers' (see Appendix B, p. 178).

Breaking bread

- Encourage children to:

    WATCH and

    LISTEN for this very special moment.

    KNOW this is all about sharing.

Questions about the Lord's Prayer and Breaking Bread

1. Agnus Dei (Lamb of God) is sung during the breaking of the bread. Is all the bread broken? What does the practice in your church symbolise?

2. The priest breaks and says the words that accompany the breaking. What does this moment in the service mean to you?

3. How can we help into an understanding and experience of the *broken* bread:

   children?

   newcomers?

   long-standing members of the congregation?

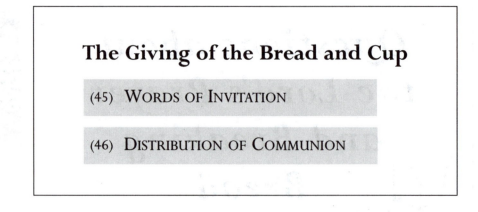

The Giving of the Bread and Cup

(45) WORDS OF INVITATION

(46) DISTRIBUTION OF COMMUNION

Jesus gives to those at the table with him. At this point in the service we come to God together. Our communion is with each other as well as with our Lord.

The giving of the bread and the cup is a solemn moment of encounter with Christ. We come with:

- wonder

- longing

- a desire for communion with the living God.

- We are sharing fellowship with him.

- We renew our commitment to him.

- We receive his life and strength.

> *It is the intense desire of God to enter into the most intimate relationship with us that forms the core of the Eucharistic celebration and Eucharistic life. God not only wants to enter human history by becoming a person who lives in a specific epoch and a specific country, but God wants to become our daily food and drink at any time and any place.*
>
> *Therefore Jesus takes bread, blesses it, breaks it, and gives it to us. And then, as we see the bread in our hands and bring it to our mouths and eat it, yes, then our eyes are opened and we recognize him.*
>
> (Henri Nouwen, *With Burning Hearts*)

There is paradox in this:

> 'We are not worthy so much as to gather up the crumbs ...'

and yet

> 'We have been counted worthy to stand in God's presence and serve him.'

The Distribution

- The moment of receiving God's blessing through the priest's hands is the climax of the service for most children. They should be helped to observe this special moment with quietness and stillness as appropriate to their age.

- Parents should be sensitive to the needs of other members of the congregation at this climax of the service, and be aware of the effect that noisy children can have on others at this time.

- The period of the distribution of Communion can be a long time for children when nothing seems to be happening for them. Have ready some activity sheets and crayons for school-age children to work on. These should be related to the theme of the day or to the actual service and enable children's minds to be creatively exercised at what can otherwise be a boring time for them, coming about an hour after the start of the service.

Younger children

- The receiving of God's blessing through the priest's hands is a special moment for the youngest children. Talk to them about it, and help to develop the sense of specialness.

- If the distribution of Communion takes a long time, small children may need to be taken for a walk, given quiet toys, or otherwise kept occupied. It is important that at this stage in the service, when their attention is short and they are getting tired, children should not become bored and disruptive.

Questions about the Invitation and the Distribution of Communion

1. How do you hold together the paradox of 'not being worthy' yet 'counted worthy'?

2. What does the receiving of bread and wine mean to you?

3. Who distributes the bread and wine in your church? How important is this to children? (There is nothing priestly about the distribution although the President will most likely want to share.)

4. How do we invite those not receiving Communion, including children, to come forward to receive a blessing?

5. What do you think newcomers and children might feel at this point? (Why not ask some of them?)

6. How can music enhance the spirit of approach?

7. How do we stop idle chatter?

8. How can we help the following to use this time well:

   children?

   newcomers?

   long-standing members of the congregation?

After Communion

(50) Appropriate sentence and hymn.

(51, 52) POST-COMMUNION PRAYER

(54) Blessing

(55) DISMISSAL

(56) MINISTERS AND PEOPLE DEPART

This part of the service enables people to:

● reflect on what they have just received;

● be sent out equipped and motivated, for living the Christian gospel in daily life.

After Communion

● In the children's Communion book *Jesus Is Here*, it says: 'The grown ups will say a prayer to thank God for feeding them. In your own words, thank Jesus for loving you and being your friend.' Encourage children to use the prayer.

Dismissal

● Say the words of dismissal from the back of the church and encourage the people to turn round and face the door. Perhaps the doors can be opened by children and attention drawn to the fact that through the worship God has prepared us to be sent out into the community. We come in to worship so that we can be sent out in the name and in the power of God.

Questions about After Communion

1. What do you think about this way of ending the service?

2. What are the implications of this part of the service for those who have not received the bread and wine?

3. How can the sense of mission, the 'being sent out', be made exciting and real for:

    children?

    newcomers?

    long-standing members of the congregation?

Finally

We hope that this book has challenged people to think, and that it will make a contribution towards the day when *every* church can display a poster similar to the one used in the Diocese of Wakefield in its porch, and live out its message in action!

The Missionary Diocese of Wakefield

A Children's Charter

Jesus said: 'Let the little children come to me and do not hinder them, for the kingdom of heaven belongs to such as these.'

- We believe children are vital members of the church today.

- We welcome children into the family of our church.

- We promise to pray faithfully for children and those who work with them.

- We promise to make the best provision we can for children to worship and to learn about the Christian faith.

Appendix A
Books quoted in the text

Peter Graystone and Eileen Turner, *A Church for All Ages*, Scripture Union, 1993.

Michelle Guiness, *A Little Kosher Seasoning*, Hodder & Stoughton, 1994.

Ishmael, *Angels with Dirty Faces,* Kingsway Publications, 1989.

Edwin Le Grice et al., *Five Instant Glorias and a Creed*, Kevin Mayhew, 1991.

Henri Nouwen, *With Burning Hearts*, Geoffrey Chapman, 1994.

Patterns for Worship, Church House Publishing, 1995.

Michael Perham, *Lively Sacrifice*, SPCK, 1992.

Michael Perry (ed.), *Church Family Worship*, Hodder & Stoughton, 1986.

Michael Perry (ed.), *The Dramatised Bible*, Marshall Pickering/Bible Society, 1989.

Report of the House of Bishops to General Synod, *Admission to Communion in Relation to Baptism and Confirmation*, GS 1212, June 1996.

Susan Sayers, *Jesus Is Here*, Kevin Mayhew, 1993.

Sharon J. Swain, *The Sermon Slot: Year 2*, SPCK, 1993.

J. H. Westerhoff III, *Bringing up Children in the Christian Faith!*, Winton Press, 1980.

Other resources referred to in text

Roly Bain, *Fools Rush In*, Marshall Pickering, 1993 (there are other books on Christian clowning also by this author).

Chris Williams and Paul Thompson, Music 'n' Mime tape *Nativity Play*, Scripture Press, 1992.

Appendix B
Children's books for use
during the church service

Books for younger children

'Talking with God' board books (Candle Books). There are *Sorry*, *Thank You* and *Please* books in this series.

'Little Fish' books (Scripture Union). There are *I'm Sorry*, *Thank you God* and *Please God* books in this series.

John Greenhalgh, *I'm Sorry God*, *Thank You God*, *God Made* and *Please God*, Scripture Union, 1987.

Graham Jeffery, *My Prayer Book*, Kevin Mayhew, 1993.

The Lord's Prayer, 'Little Bible Window Prayers', Nelson Word Ltd, 1994.

Linda Parry, *Father in Heaven*, the Lord's Prayer in the 'Friends with God' series, Hunt & Thorpe, 1994.

Children's Holy Communion books

Susan Sayers, *Jesus Is Here*, Kevin Mayhew, 1993.
(This has lovely 'busy' pictures which will capture a child's imagination. The text is modified in places to meet the needs of those not receiving the sacraments.)

The Lord is Here, Collins, 1981.
(The Rite A (or Rite B) Holy Communion Service text divided into sections with appropriate headings and bold pictures.)

Bells Are Ringing, Church Information Office, 1978.
(This is now out of print but has cartoon pictures suited to the Catholic tradition.)

Kathleen Crawford, *My Communion Book*, Church House Publishing, 1995.
(A book specially written for the under-7s.)

Appendix C
Pew packs for children aged 3–6 years

Pew packs are packs of materials (a theme in a bag) which can be available for the use of 3- to 6-year-old children who attend worship in church. The packs provide interesting, stimulating materials, all related to the Christian faith, to which children can return at those times in the service when their attention is not being focused on the action, ritual or music of the worship. The purpose of children being present in the service is that they may absorb the atmosphere and at different points in the service have their attention focused on what is happening. This is difficult for young children at those times in the worship when it is all 'words, words, words'.

Pew packs are not to be given to a child to keep him or her quiet so that he or she can then be ignored.

Example: The Lost Sheep

The pew pack could contain:

- A book which tells the story (there are several available in Christian bookshops).

- A photocopied activity book to colour and take home.

- A template of a sheep and some plain paper and crayons (wax crayons, not felt-tips for small children).

- A jigsaw puzzle (e.g. Boots' 12-piece puzzle, 'Sheep').

- A small woolly toy sheep to handle and to hide.

- A sheep mask to take home, enlarged from the Palm Tree *Things to Make and Do*, Book 2.

Appendix D

Selection of songs suitable for all-age worship

The Hymns and Songs List compiled by David Barker (Hodder & Stoughton, 1992) is useful. It suggests hymns and songs for each Sunday, following the ASB lectionary, but not particularly for all-age services.

Hymns Ancient and Modern, New Standard (The Canterbury Press, 1983) has a useful index of hymns for the Sunday themes in the ASB lectionary, which includes traditional and more modern hymns.

Hymns Old and New (Anglican Edition) (Kevin Mayhew, 1996) has an 'Index of Uses', suggesting hymns and songs for every Sunday of the year.

The lists below suggest songs and hymns particularly suitable when children are present in an all-age service, because they have repetitive words or choruses which can be announced, and give to children who cannot read the opportunity to join in.

Key

CP	*Children's Praise*, Marshall Pickering, 1991.
JP1/JP2	*Junior Praise 1* and *Junior Praise 2* (Nos 302–503), Marshall Pickering, 1986, 1992.
SAL1/SAL2	*Sing-a-long Song Book*, Books 1 and 2, Integrity Music, 1991, 1992.

List of songs

Alleluia, alleluia, give thanks to the risen Lord (JP2/CP2)

Bind us together (JP17)

Bless the Lord, O my soul (JP19)

Come and praise the Lord our King (JP34/CP13)

Give me oil in my lamp (JP50/274)

Go tell it on the mountain (JP65)

Happy birthday, Jesus (SAL 2-141)

The heavens are telling (CP165)

He's got the whole world in his hands (JP78/CP62/SAL1-55)

I have decided to follow Jesus (JP98)

I'm going to shine, shine, shine (JP392)

In the beginning (CP93)

I will sing, I will sing a song unto the Lord (JP126)

Jesus is a friend of mine (JP136)

King of kings and Lord of lords (JP148)

Kum ba yah (JP149)

Make way, make way (JP427)

Oh, oh, oh, how good is the Lord (JP180/CP133)

Stand up, clap hands, shout thank you Lord (JP225)

Thank you Lord for this fine day (JP232/CP160)

There's a song of exultation (JP247)

This is the day that the Lord has made (JP255/CP172/SAL2-180)

What a mighty God we serve (SAL 2-95)

What a wonderful saviour (CP33)

We have a king who rides a donkey (JP264/CP180)

When I needed a neighbour were you there? (JP275)

For very simple songs, many with actions, sung to familiar tunes (nursery rhymes, folk tunes etc.) see the following books:

David C. C. Cook, *100 Action Songs for Toddlers*, Scripture Union, 1989.

David C. C. Cook, *100 Action Songs for Preschoolers*, Scripture Union, 1991.

Peter Churchill, *Feeling Good: Songs of Wonder and Worship for the Under-5's*, Church House Publishing/National Society, 1994.

Twenty Hymns from Ancient and Modern (Revised) *which have repetition etc.*

All creatures of our God and King (172)

All glory, laud, and honour (98)

All things bright and beautiful (442)

Eternal Father, strong to save (487)

For all the saints (527)

For the beauty of the earth (171)

Good Christian men, rejoice and sing (603)

Hail the day that sees him rise (147)

Hark! the herald angels sing (60)

Jesus Christ is risen today (134)

Let all the world in every corner sing (375)

O come, all ye faithful (59)

Onward, Christian soldiers (629)

Praise, my soul, the King of heaven (365)

Praise, O praise our God and King (481)

Rejoice, the Lord is King (216)

Ride on, ride on in majesty (99)

Thou, whose almighty word (266)

When morning gilds the sky (223)

We plough the fields and scatter (483)

and there are many more!

Appendix E

Choosing materials for children's groups running at the same time as part of the adult service ('Junior Church')

When choosing the Junior Church materials which most suit the needs of a parish, certain criteria need to be applied to the selection process.

Considerations when selecting Junior Church materials:

Are we looking for:

- separate units week by week or continuity? Do children attend regularly or not?
- dated/undated material? Do you have a monthly Family Service and so only have a group three weeks out of four?
- lengthy/brief material? How much time have you got with the children?
- supplementary material? If so, what kind do we want?
- economical/more expensive material? How much money do/can you spend on material and supportive resources?

Other considerations

- age spread per class?
- preparation time available?
- use of photocopier?

Teaching materials

Details of different commercially produced schemes and projects are given below.

Bible in Life curriculum for 2- to 14-year-olds, published quarterly by Nova Distribution Ltd, 29 Milber Industrial Estate, Newton Abbot, Devon TQ12 4SG. (*Not linked to ASB lectionary themes or to worship of any denomination.*)

Faithquest, a four-year syllabus for Sunday schools and children's groups presented in four age-bands, Collins, 1991. *(Not directly linked to ASB lectionary themes or to Parish Communion.)*

The Feast, undated children's teaching resources, published by Word Curriculum, Nelson Word Ltd, Milton Keynes, at regular intervals. *(Claims to be the first charismatic scheme to be published.)*

First Steps (1987); *Step This Way* 1 and 2 (1992, 1993); *Steps and Stones,* 1, 2, 3, 4, National Society/Church House Publishing, 1983. *(Not directly linked to ASB lectionary themes.)*

Leslie J. Francis and Marian Carter, *The Word for all God's Family,* Gracewing, 1996. *(Projects on Scripture based on the ASB lectionary.)*

Getting to Know God, 1 and 2, a two-year teaching course. *(Not directly linked to ASB lectionary themes or to Rite A.)*

Mable Hayes, *Teaching Christianity,* a four-year course for children aged 7–11 for church schools and church groups, Mowbray, 1982. *(Not directly linked to ASB lectionary themes or to Parish Communion.)*

Diana Morgan, *Growing in Faith,* ASB Years One and Two, Leaders' Resource Books 1 and 2 (half the year in each), Canterbury Press: Year Two (1991); Year One (1992). *(ASB lectionary-based, assuming children are part of ASB Rite A Eucharist from Offertory onwards.)*

Partners in Learning, presented in themes each lasting four weeks. Published in three volumes each year by the National Christian Education Council. *(Bible-based material based on the Christian year.)*

SALT ('Sharing and Learning Together'), teaching material for children aged 3–14, with all-age worship material, published quarterly by Scripture Union.

Susan Sayers, *Springboard to Worship,* Kevin Mayhew, 1989, and *Including the Children* (Kevin Mayhew, 1990). *(Ideas, resources, activities and photocopiable activity sheets based on ASB lectionary.* First Fruits (1996) *and* Children Too (1995) *are also based on ASB themes.)*

Teaching Christianity, 'Instant Art' series, Palm Tree, 1991.

TREK, undated material for children aged 3–6 and 7–10, with supplementary material (badges, balloons etc.), published by CPAS.

Additional material for leaders of children aged 3-6 years

Bible Stories and Activities for the Under 5's, six books, CPAS, 1991–94.

Peter Churchill, *Feeling Good: Songs of Worship and Wonder for Fives and Under*, National Society/Church House Publishing, 1994.

First Class: A Child's First Lessons in Knowing God, TNT Ministries St Matthew's Press, 1993.

Leslie J. Francis and Nicola M. Slee, *Teddy Horsley Stories* – various titles, NCEC,1987.

Janet Gaukroger, *Bible Stuff: Spiritual Teaching for Under Fives That's Fun*, CPAS, 1996.

Here's One I Made Earlier, Scripture Union, 1995. Crafts for 3–11's.

Praise Paint and Play: Christian Fun for the Under 5's, National Society/Church House Publishing, 1995.